# ORTHO'S®

S0-AFD-334

## 50 Quick
# Home
## Improvements

Editor: Karen K. Johnson
Writers: Sharon Ross and Dave Toht
Illustrators: Tony Davis, Brian Jensen, and Pamela Wattenmaker

Meredith® Books
Des Moines, Iowa

Ortho® Books
An imprint of Meredith® Books

*Ortho's 50 Quick Home Improvements*
Solaris Book Development Team
Publisher: Robert B. Loperena
Editorial Director: Christine Jordan
Managing Editor: Sally W. Smith
Acquisitions Editors: Robert J. Beckstrom,
    Michael D. Smith
Publisher's Assistant: Joni Christiansen
Graphics Coordinator: Sally J. French
Editorial Coordinator: Cass Dempsey
Production Manager: Linda Bouchard

**Meredith Book Development Team**
Project Editor: Larry Erickson
Art Director: Tom Wegner
Copy Chief: Catherine Hamrick
Copy and Production Editor: Terri Fredrickson
Contributing Proofreader: Debra Morris Smith
Electronic Production Coordinator: Paula Forest
Editorial and Design Assistants: Judy Bailey, Kaye Chabot,
    Treesa Landry, Karen Schirm, Kathleen Stevens
Production Director: Douglas M. Johnston
Production Manager: Pam Kvitne
Assistant Prepress Manager: Marjorie J. Schenkelberg

**Additional Editorial Contributions from
    Greenleaf Publishing**
Publishing Director: Dave Toht
Associate Editor: Steve Cory
Assistant Editor: Rebecca JonMichaels
Editorial Art Director: Jean DeVaty
Design: Melanie Lawson Design
Illustrations: Tony Davis
Additional Photography: Dan Stultz
Technical Consultant: Michael Clark

**Meredith® Books**
Editor in Chief: James D. Blume
Design Director: Matt Strelecki
Managing Editor: Gregory H. Kayko
Executive Ortho Editor: Benjamin W. Allen

Director, Sales & Marketing, Retail: Michael A. Peterson
Director, Sales & Marketing, Special Markets:
    Rita McMullen
Director, Sales & Marketing, Home & Garden Center
    Channel: Ray Wolf
Director, Operations: George A. Susral

Vice President, General Manager: Jamie L. Martin

**Meredith Publishing Group**
President, Publishing Group: Christopher M. Little
Vice President, Consumer Marketing & Development:
    Hal Oringer

**Meredith Corporation**
Chairman and Chief Executive Officer: William T. Kerr

Chairman of the Executive Committee: E.T. Meredith III

**Additional Photographers**
Ed Gohlich: 72
John North Holtorf: cover
Jon Jensen: 54
Jennifer Jordan: 4, 24

All of us at Ortho® Books are dedicated to providing you
with the information and ideas you need to enhance your
home and garden. We welcome your comments and
suggestions about this book. Write to us at:
Meredith Corporation
Ortho Books
1716 Locust St.
Des Moines, IA 50309–3023

**Note to the Readers:** Due to differing conditions, tools,
and individual skills, Meredith Corporation assumes no
responsibility for any damages, injuries suffered, or losses
incurred as a result of following the information published
in this book. Before beginning any project, review the
instructions carefully, and if any doubts or questions remain,
consult local experts or authorities. Because codes and
regulations vary greatly, you always should check with
authorities to ensure that your project complies with all
applicable local codes and regulations. Always read and
observe all of the safety precautions provided by
manufacturers of any tools, equipment, or supplies,
and follow all accepted safety procedures.

# WELCOMING ROOMS 4

# WORKING ROOMS 24

# PERSONAL ROOMS 52

# CURB APPEAL 72

*With a little effort, you can dress up your entryway and living room
to extend a warm, personal welcome. Molding, tile, and paint
projects look terrific, and they're easier than most people expect.*

# WELCOMING ROOMS

Most homes, whether new or old, have room for improvement. Often a small change, such as adding shelves or painting a wall in a new way, can make a surprising difference. Suddenly, your home is more attractive, functional, and comfortable. And most projects require only a little money, some elbow grease, and a weekend or two. This book features 50 relatively inexpensive projects that add style, convenience, and ease to a home. They range from sprucing up rooms with trim moldings to boosting the efficiency of a closet.

The book begins with fresh, fun ideas for updating public rooms—the entryway, living room, family room, and dining room. Then it offers home improvement tips for the kitchen and bathrooms, the bedrooms, and, finally, the exterior of your home.

# TILE AN ENTRYWAY

Ceramic tile—an attractive, durable, and easy-care floor—will lend sophistication to an entryway previously floored with sheet vinyl or vinyl tiles. You also can use tile to dress up a kitchen or bathroom floor. The floor must be solid, or tiles will crack in time. If you feel the floor springing as you jump on it, take steps to strengthen it; adding a layer of ½-inch plywood may do the trick. At the same time, make sure that your future tile surface will not be more than ½ inch higher than any other floor surface that it abuts, or the step down will look awkward. Once the subsurface is sound, it will take two days to tile a typical entryway.

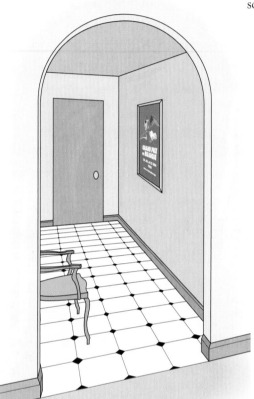

*A ceramic tile entry floor will add style to your home and give you a long-lasting surface that is easy to clean.*

## WHAT YOU'LL NEED

**MATERIALS:** tile (buy an additional 15 percent to allow for waste); grout; thin-set mortar or floor tile adhesive (consult a dealer for the best product for your situation); plastic tile spacers (choose your grout width); thresholds; sheets of plywood subflooring; 6d nails or 1⅝-inch screws, if needed.

**TOOLS:** broad knife or other scraping tool; hand or power sander; tape measure; chalk line; long straightedge; tile cutter; notched trowel (ask dealer for right size for your material); tile cutter; tile nippers; framing square; knee pads or kneeling pad; rubber mallet; flat 3-foot-square piece of plywood; sponge; laminated grout float; rags.

## PREPARE THE FLOOR

You can install ceramic tile directly over any clean, dry, level surface in sound condition. But to keep the floor from getting too high, you will want to rip up the existing flooring, if possible. If your existing floor is old linoleum, it may well contain asbestos, and you should leave it in place. Asbestos is not harmful when encased in a solid material in sound condition, but you risk releasing the fibers into the air if you remove it.

Remove existing thresholds, as

The most visible wall

Wall is out of square, but job is planned to avoid slivers

Lay the last tile on top for measuring

A piece of plywood with two factory edges makes a good square well as the base shoe or baseboards. You may need to cut your door. Ask a tile dealer to determine whether or not you need plywood underlayment and to recommend the correct primer, adhesive, and grout for your floor.

Scrape the floor as clean as possible with a broad knife. Sand down ridges and rough up any glossy surface. Vacuum the debris and damp-mop the floor to remove all traces of dust. If you are installing a new underlayment, apply construction adhesive to the back, lay it down, and nail or screw it in place every 3 to 4 inches around the perimeter and every 6 to 12 inches along each floor joist. Allow ¼-inch expansion joints between the underlayment and the wall. Cover the wood, including the edges, with the recommended primer and then fill the joints with setting material.

## LAY OUT THE JOB

Find the center of the floor by measuring the halfway mark on each wall. Snap chalk lines between the centers on opposite walls. The lines should cross at true 90-degree angles. Check with a framing square to be sure. Lay test rows of dry tiles along the chalk lines in all four directions, allowing for the spaces between the tiles. If the space between the wall and the last tile is less than half a tile on each end, adjust the layout so you have a full tile on one end and a larger partial tile on the other.

Check to see if your room is square. If not, there will be at least one wall where the tiles will be narrower at one end than at the other. Plan so that this happens on a wall that is not very visible. Or split the difference so that two or more walls have tiles that vary in width but not by very much.

Snap chalk layout lines that are perfectly square to each other. Plan so that you can finish the job in one day; remember not to step or kneel on tiles until they have fully set. Usually, the best course is to start in one corner and work outward, pyramid fashion. To make sure that you have a straight line, lay a long straightedge on the floor and weight it down so it will not move if you bump it.

## MIX AND SPREAD THE ADHESIVE

Depending on your tile and your subsurface, you may be able to use premixed floor tile adhesive. Chances are, however, that your dealer will recommend a dry-mix thin-set mortar or adhesive. One type has latex additives in the dry mix, so you need to add only water. The type that requires adding a liquid latex will be more expensive but stronger.

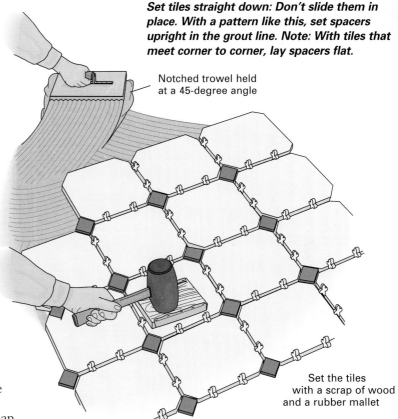

*Set tiles straight down: Don't slide them in place. With a pattern like this, set spacers upright in the grout line. Note: With tiles that meet corner to corner, lay spacers flat.*

Notched trowel held at a 45-degree angle

Set the tiles with a scrap of wood and a rubber mallet

Mix according to directions—usually to a toothpastelike consistency, wait 10 minutes, then stir again. For a small job, you can do this by hand, but if you have a lot of mixing to do, use a mixing attachment on a drill.

Scoop the adhesive onto the floor with a notched trowel. Holding the trowel at a 45-degree angle, spread the adhesive up to but not over the chalk lines. Cover an area that you can finish in 20 to 30 minutes.

## SET THE TILE

Set each tile straight down with a slight twisting motion. Do not slide it into place. Then press firmly into place with your hands and tap with a rubber mallet to set. As you work, make sure the tiles are level with one another. (Grout will not mask unevenness but will actually make it more apparent than it is now.)

Keep everything clean as you work. Wipe the face of the tile with a damp rag. Set the next tile the same way. Insert plastic tile

## TILE AN ENTRYWAY
*continued*

Once all the tiles are laid, do not let anyone walk on the floor for at least a day. Under humid conditions, you may need to wait longer. To ensure that the adhesive will dry, direct a fan to blow over the surface.

laminated grout float

### GROUT AND CLEAN

Remove the spacers. If recommended, apply grout release to the tiles. Mix the grout according to directions. Spread it diagonally over the tiles with a grout float, working it well into the joints by holding the float nearly flat and pushing down as you move it in sweeping arcs. Sweep across all the joint lines in at least two directions. Work small sections at a time. Then tip the float up and use it like a squeegee to remove the excess grout from the tiles without removing it from the joints. Move diagonally to the lines. Let the grout stand until the joints are firm. Wipe the tiles clean with a damp sponge without removing grout from the joints. Let the grout set for 72 hours, then wash the floor with clear water and polish the surface with a soft cloth. Seal the grout and the tile as the tile dealer recommends.

spacers between the tiles as you work. Move or leave them in place to be grouted over, if desired. After every few tiles, check your work to be sure it is square and level. It may help to use a flat piece of plywood about 3 feet square; set it on the tiles you've been working with and tap gently if any unevenness is detected.

Mark for straight cuts by measuring or by holding a tile in place. Don't forget to take the width of the grout line into account. Set the tile in a tile cutter, butted up against the guide and positioned so the cutting wheel will cut your line. Score a single line by pressing down and sliding the handle forward. Snap the cut by pushing down hard on the handle. If you need to cut a number of tiles to the same size, use the adjustable guide. Use tile nippers to cut tiles to fit curved shapes.

### INSTALL THE THRESHOLDS

Reinstall the base shoe or baseboard molding, taking care not to drive nails into the tile or the grout line. Purchase appropriate thresholds. For example, a beveled metal threshold makes a smooth transition if the two floors are not level with each other. If you are butting a floor to an oak wood floor, an oak threshold is a good choice.

Cut a metal threshold with tin snips. Use a miter box for a wood threshold. Install with decorative screws.

*Make the transition between flooring materials with a simple strip of metal threshold fastened in place with screws or tacks.*

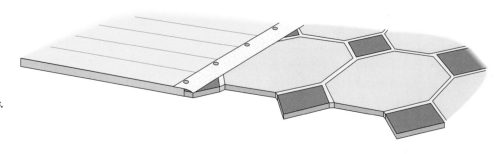

# ADD A HALL SHELF

Some entryways cannot comfortably accommodate a console table or chest. Remedy this by hanging a shelf with decorative brackets on the wall at the height of a countertop or a tabletop. It offers a convenient place to lay keys and gloves. Hang a mirror or picture over it for an attractive accent in an otherwise empty space. Once you have purchased the parts, this shelf will take about half a day to build and finish.

*A simple entry shelf gives you a place to keep a notebook or keys within easy reach without dominating your entryway.*

## WHAT YOU'LL NEED

**MATERIALS:** Two decorative brackets; 1×8 or 1×10 board for shelf; fluted screen molding to cover three edges of shelf; 4d finishing nails; brads for attaching molding; wood glue; screws for attaching brackets; wood putty; wood plugs; paint or stain with a polyurethane finish.

**TOOLS:** tape measure; miter box or power miter box (rentable); stud finder; drill; level; pencil; hammer; nail set; paintbrush.

## PLAN FOR A SHELF THAT FITS

Determine the shelf location and size. It should be near the front door and coat closet, but not in the path of the door's swing. Track the full arc of the door's swing to determine which sections of wall you must avoid. Have a helper hold a board in place to make sure it will not impede traffic.

## ASSEMBLE THE PARTS

Look for decorative brackets at an architectural salvage yard or a renovation supply house. (Shelf brackets purchased from a building-supply retailer are less attractive than antique brackets.) Exterior brackets and corbels work well, too. Take your treasures home and clean up and refinish them, if necessary.

Cut a board or a piece of plywood to your dimensions. Use a miter box or power miter box to cut the edging pieces, and attach them to three edges of the shelf with glue and small brads.

## HANG THE SHELF

Use a level and a pencil to mark a line showing the bottom edge of the shelf. Locate the wall studs along this line with a stud finder. If possible, attach the brackets directly to the studs. If not, use the nailer arrangement shown below. No more than one-sixth of the length of the shelf should cantilever off each bracket.

Attach the shelf to the brackets with 4d finishing nails. Countersink the nail heads, using a nail set, and fill the holes with wood putty. Drill pilot holes and counterbore holes for the screws, and insert decorative plugs. Apply two coats of high-gloss paint, or stain and apply a coat of polyurethane finish.

*Assemble by cutting and trimming the shelf first. Then build the support so the brackets are set in 4–6 inches from the shelf ends.*

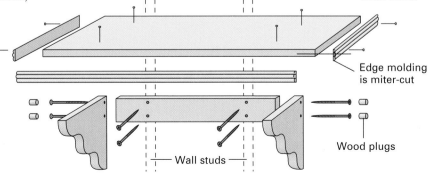

Edge molding is miter-cut

Wood plugs

Wall studs

# UPGRADE WITH MOLDINGS

Moldings add depth and elegance to a room. They also accent its best features, helping trick the eye into seeing the space as wider or narrower, longer or shorter than it actually is. With good tools and some patience, you can install professional-looking moldings. As a very general rule, count on installing about five pieces of molding per hour.

*A variety of moldings make for a richly textured look. A three-part base molding is mirrored by an elaborate crown molding at the ceiling (see pages 12–13). A horizontal chair rail located about 4 feet above the floor allows for different wall treatments.*

## WHAT YOU'LL NEED

**MATERIALS:** moldings (measure for each piece and buy a variety of lengths); 3d or 4d finishing nails for thin moldings, 6d or 8d finishing nails for thicker pieces; construction adhesive; wood filler; latex/silicone caulk; paint or stain with a polyurethane finish.

**TOOLS:** tape measure; pencil; chalk line (for chair rail); miter box and backsaw or power miter box (rentable); squeeze clamps; coping saw; sanding block; stud finder; drill and ⅛-inch drill bit; putty knife; hammer and nail set or electric nailer (rentable); paintbrush.

## WAYS TO USE MOLDINGS

There are scores of ways to use molding to enhance a room. Mount crown or cove moldings at ceiling lines. Put chair rails and picture moldings or other trims at soffit height or at midwall. Mask corners and seams with corner moldings and highlight fireplace mantels with crown or cornice moldings and other trims. Dress up cabinets (*as in the picture above*) by adding fluted edge molding to the shelves and installing casings with decorative corner blocks. You also can cover the lower half of a wall with vertical tongue-and-groove wainscoting.

For a quaint effect, mount picture molding (it has a rounded top and was originally designed for hanging pictures with clips and wires) on the wall below but not touching the ceiling. Or mount them on the ceiling behind the crown or cove molding.

To make more lavish moldings, build up layers of stock moldings. For example, create a custom crown molding by mounting base molding a few inches below the ceiling. Trim its bottom edge with picture molding and mount the crown molding on its top edge. Any number of combinations is possible.

## PLANNING HINTS

■ Keep the molding pattern appropriate to the room's style and purpose.
■ Keep the molding width in proportion to the size of the room.
■ Align low wall moldings with the bottom of windows or a major piece of furniture.
■ Align high wall moldings with the tops of windows and doors or with a major piece of furniture.
■ Place chair rails and wainscot caps 26–30 inches above the floor.
■ It may save time and effort to stain or paint the wood before cutting it. That way, you will have to touch up only the cut ends and the filled holes after the molding is installed.

## MITER AND COPED CUTS

Wear safety goggles and make practice cuts on scrap material before you begin. Smooth the cut edges with a sanding block.

A miter cut is a 45-degree angle-cut that lets pieces fit together at corners. Mark the molding at the angle's longest point and set it in the miter box. It is important to hold the molding in the correct way in the box; experiment with scrap pieces before you cut a large piece. Base molding goes in right side up, as if the bottom of the box were the floor and the back were the wall. Lay door and window casings right side up in the bottom of the box, as if the bottom were the wall. Hold the molding firmly in place or secure with C-clamps and pads. Here are some tips.
■ Outside corner base moldings: Cut the right-hand corner from left to right. After cutting, the right piece is the right corner. Cut the left-hand corner from right to left. The left piece is the left corner.
■ For an inside corner on base moldings: Cut the left-hand corner from left to right. After cutting, the left piece is the left corner. Cut the right-hand corner from right to left. The right piece is the right corner.

A coped joint is a butt joint used for inside corners and is often the only way to ensure a tight joint. It is particularly useful for base molding. It is a bit more challenging than an inside miter cut but not as difficult as it may

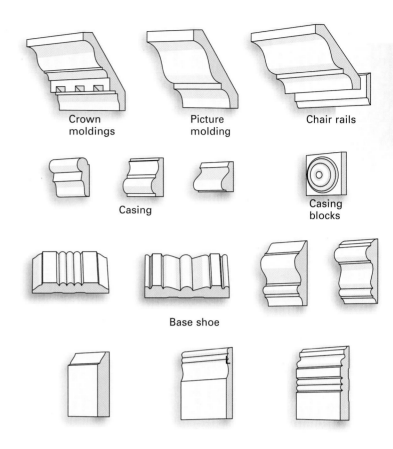

Crown moldings

Picture molding

Chair rails

Casing

Casing blocks

Base shoe

appear. Cut the first piece at a 90-degree angle so it fits flush to the adjoining wall. Then cut the second piece to fit the face profile of the flush piece (*see instructions for coped cuts on page 13*).

## NAIL IN PLACE

Before you start nailing, find solid wood behind the wall surface into which you can drive nails. Locate studs (usually 16 inches apart) with a stud finder; at the bottom and top of walls, there will be horizontal plates, as well. Drive experimental nails and mark stud locations with light pencil marks.

Install molding piece by piece, working around the room. Drive small nails every few feet along the chalk line before you begin. The molding rests on these nails while you glue and nail it to the wall.

If installing synthetic molding, coat the back or nailing edges with the recommended adhesive, press in place, and nail. Nail wood moldings in place with or without construction adhesive, as you prefer. Drive the nails through predrilled holes wherever the molding crosses a stud. They should go through a part of the molding that sits flat against the wall and ¾ inch into the studs. Countersink the nail heads the distance of their diameter. Fill with wood putty that matches your stain or fill, sand, and paint.

*In addition to the familiar colonial and ranch moldings, vintage moldings like these offer new possibilities for upgrading a room.*

# CROWN A ROOM REGALLY

*Molding added to the wall can make a simple crown molding more complex.*

With crown molding, you can add a new look to a room in a short time. A variety of attractive crown molding types are available, and you can enhance plain crown molding by adding other pieces of stock molding—colonial stop, for instance—to the wall or ceiling surfaces.

The job requires some precise cutting, but if you treat each piece with care, your efforts will be well rewarded. Have at least one sturdy stepladder—better yet, make a platform out of a plank and two stable sawhorses. You will need a helper to assist with the long pieces. As a general rule, count on installing about four pieces of crown molding per hour.

## PLAN THE JOB

On a piece of paper, make a diagram of the pieces, planning so that as few pieces as possible will have to be miter-cut on both ends. If you have a wall longer than the longest piece of molding, plan the location of a butt joint so it will not be highly visible. Start working in the least visible part of the room because you will probably make better joints once you've had some practice.

Hold a scrap piece of crown molding in place and determine where you will put the nails. Be sure you will drive into solid wood—the ceiling plate at the top of the wall, wall studs, or ceiling joists. For larger crown molding, it may make sense to

## WHAT YOU'LL NEED

**MATERIALS:** molding (measure for each piece); 6d or 8d finishing nails; wood filler; paint or stain with a polyurethane finish.

**TOOLS:** power miter box (rentable) or high-quality miter box with backsaw; squeeze clamps; coping saw; knife; stud finder; drill and ⅛-inch drill bit; putty knife; sandpaper; hammer and nail set or electric nailer (rentable).

install a horizontal 2×2 in the corner to provide an easy nailing surface.

Crown molding is somewhat difficult to work with, especially if it is wide. Walls and ceilings are seldom perfectly square and true, so often cuts must be fine-tuned. And because

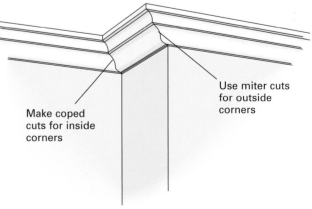

Make coped cuts for inside corners

Use miter cuts for outside corners

the joints will be more visible than with base molding, they must be close to perfect. So spend some time practicing on scrap pieces, cutting them as shown on these pages and holding them in place. Don't start cutting the real stuff until you feel very comfortable with your skills.

## MEASURE AND MITER-CUT

When preparing to cut crown molding, set it upside down, as if the bottom of the miter box were the ceiling and the back of the box were the wall. For outside corners, miter-cut both pieces. Cut the left-hand corner from left to right. After cutting, the right piece is the left corner. Cut the right-hand corner from right to left. The left piece is the right corner. For inside corners, you can try miter-cutting both pieces (*see the illustrations at right*), but unless your walls are perfectly square, you will end up with imperfect joints. A better solution—and it doesn't take as long as you may think—is to make a coped cut.

## MAKE A COPED CORNER

Cut the first piece square and install it tight to the corner. Then miter the second piece. Cut a right-hand piece from left to right; cut a left-hand piece from right to left. As with all miter cuts, place the molding upside down in the miter box, as if the back of the box were the wall. If possible, have the cope-cut piece be longer than needed so that if you make a mistake you can try again.

Next, use a coping saw to make a cut that follows the miter cut along the face of the

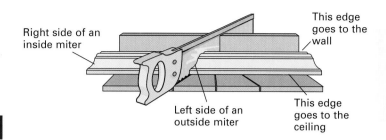

Right side of an inside miter

Left side of an outside miter

This edge goes to the wall

This edge goes to the ceiling

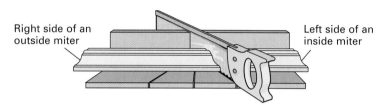

Right side of an outside miter

Left side of an inside miter

*As you cut the miters, check carefully that your work is positioned for the cut you want.*

molding. This new cut duplicates the profile of the molding. When making the coped cut, angle the blade back a bit. This process, called back-cutting, ensures that the face of the coped molding fits tightly against the face of the adjacent molding. Cut too much rather than too little from the back of the piece, since only the face will be visible. Remove any excess material with a utility knife, taking care not to damage the face of the molding. Hold the piece in place, to see if it fits tightly. If not, you may need to recut.

Because walls and ceilings are often out of square, you may have to fine-tune the joints. Sometimes it helps to use small shims at the ceiling to bring one piece down a little. Other times, you may need to shave the top or bottom edge of a piece to make it fit flush against an imperfect surface.

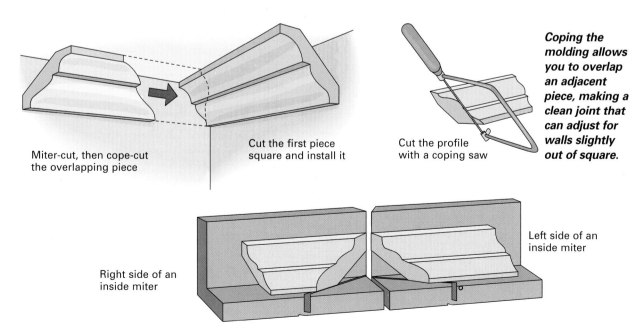

Miter-cut, then cope-cut the overlapping piece

Cut the first piece square and install it

Cut the profile with a coping saw

*Coping the molding allows you to overlap an adjacent piece, making a clean joint that can adjust for walls slightly out of square.*

Right side of an inside miter

Left side of an inside miter

# INSTALL RECESSED LIGHTS

Recessed lights are unobtrusive, so you can add one or more without significantly changing the look of a room. They also are very inexpensive and relatively easy to install. They can provide task lighting on a specific surface like a desktop or accent lighting to brighten a dim spot; they can wash down a wall or highlight

*A single recessed light can focus on one specific area; a series of lights will brighten a whole room.*

a treasured object. A group of recessed lights will brighten a whole room.

Work safely: If you are not sure of yourself, hire an electrician to run the cable. Be sure power is shut off at the service panel before you work with existing wiring. Once electrical cable is run, it will take an hour or two to install a fixture.

## WHAT YOU'LL NEED

**MATERIALS:** recessed housings (cans) with trims and bulbs; electrical cable; junction box; twist-type wire connectors; electrical tape.

**TOOLS:** graph paper; stud finder; stepladder; tape measure; keyhole saw; lineman's pliers; wire strippers.

## PLAN THE LOCATIONS

For task and accent lighting, simply look at your space and decide where you need more light. Flooding a room with consistent overall light calls for evenly spaced downlights across the ceiling. Place them approximately 6 to 8 feet apart and 3 feet in from the wall; adjust this spacing so they fit between two joists (use a stud finder to locate the joists). Better yet, have a lighting showroom design the layout. Most provide free design service if you buy the light fixtures from the showroom.

## TYPES OF CANS

You need a housing, called a "can," for each light, plus the trim and bulb to go with it. Most dealers have good displays that show what each style of trim and bulb does best. Buy a housing rated for use in remodeling. Several methods of attaching to the ceiling are available; be sure you understand how you will install your fixture before you buy it. Check to see that the can will take bulbs you want to use—some take only 60-watt bulbs. If your ceiling joists are smaller than 2×8s, you will need a special small-space can.

Various types of trims are available for different looks. Cans that are black on the inside will throw a more subtle light. Eyeball-type fixtures can be swiveled to focus on a particular spot. There are two types.

■ I.C. (insulated ceiling) housing: This indicates a can that can be installed in insulated areas. Insulation can touch the sides and top of the can.

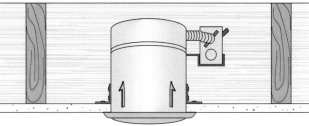

I.C. (insulated ceiling) fixture can have insulation touching it

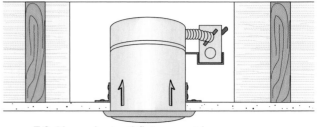

T.C. (thermal cutout) fixture must have open space around it or it will overheat

■ T.C. (thermal cutout), or non-I.C. housing: This can is intended for uninsulated areas. If it's installed where insulation is present, the insulation must be kept at least 3 inches away from all sides of the can, and none should be installed over the top. Otherwise, the can will overheat, and a thermal switch will deaden the fixture or cause it to blink.

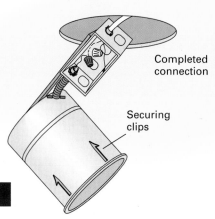

Completed connection

Securing clips

*After connecting the wires, carefully push the can into the opening and secure the clips that hold it to the ceiling material.*

## PREPARE THE OPENING

Before you begin, check your local electrical code requirements. If you are unsure of your ability to install a downlight, hire a licensed electrician to do the job.

Be sure that the hole will fall between joists. The fixture will come with a circular template; use it as a guide for drawing a circle on the ceiling. If you have a series of lights to install, draw all the circles before you begin cutting. Cut out the opening with a keyhole saw. Work carefully, so you won't have to patch your ceiling afterward.

Shut off the electrical power at the service panel. The can must be connected with supply wire rated at 90° C. (The supply wire in most houses built before 1985 is rated 60° C.) Replace the supply wire, if necessary. Make the correct connections in an existing junction box or switch box, taking care not to overload a box with too many wires; install a new junction box, if needed.

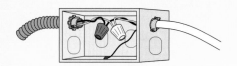

Black wire to black wire, white to white, and ground to ground

Find a way to fish electrical cable from an existing switch up through the walls into the ceiling and down to the hole. If you have access to an unfinished attic floor above the ceiling, that will make your work easier. Running cable parallel to the joists is fairly easy. But if you need to run across the joists, you may have to cut a small hole in the ceiling at each joist, then notch the joist to make a path for the cable. Install a protective metal plate wherever the cable is in danger of

having a nail poked into it. Leave at least a foot of extra cable hanging down through the hole to make it easy to hook to the fixtures.

For more than one downlight, you may need to install a readily accessible junction box in the ceiling and run the cable to it. Then pull a cable from the junction box down through each hole. Or you may be able to use the fixtures themselves as junction boxes and run cable from fixture to fixture. In that case, leave a series of cables running from hole to hole.

## MAKE THE ELECTRICAL CONNECTION

Wire each outlet box by connecting the wires (black to black, white to white) with twist-type wire connectors. Connect the green ground wire to the ground wire in the power source. Tuck the wires into the box and close.

## INSTALL CAN AND TRIM

There are several ways to install the cans, depending on the type. For some, install a mounting frame before you hook the wiring, then slide the can into the mounting frame and secure it with a screw. Others use clips that simply push up to secure the can to wallboard or plaster. Follow the manufacturer's directions to install the trim. Some types use a reflector, as well.

Install the correct bulb: Using higher wattage than recommended will dangerously heat your wiring. Often a higher-wattage floodlight can be used instead of a lower-wattage standard bulb.

# COLOR WASH A WALL

Color washing is one of the most effective faux paint finishes and one of the easiest. The technique involves building up thin layers of translucent color, one on top of another, to produce a subtle, dappled effect. The rich, mellow look complements country rooms and other informal settings. Color washing has one drawback—it's messy. Cover the floor and furniture with plastic sheeting (taped to the baseboards) and tarps. Count on spending two days preparing and painting an average bedroom.

Typically, color-washed walls have a white, off-white, or light-colored base coat. Cover this base with a minimum of two or three layers of paint thinned to a wash consistency. The washes can be the same color—one that contrasts with the base coat and gains depth from being layered over itself—or they can be tints and shades from the same color family in the gradations shown on a paint sample card. An example is different yellows layered over one another on top of a warm white, ivory, or pale yellow base coat. Or use colors that are related—for example, a pale blue base coat washed with layers of red-violet, violet, and blue-violet. The thinner the paint and the more coats applied, the richer the look.

Experiment on scrap pieces of wood if you are not sure which look is best for you. Choose light color over dark color, or dark over light. Remember that you will see more of the wash than the base coat.

*A color-washed wall enriches a room with interesting mixes of hues and delicate hints of texture.*

## WHAT YOU'LL NEED

**MATERIALS:** spackle and/or spray-on crack sealer; primer; latex or alkyd interior paints; polyurethane finish, if desired; mineral spirits, if needed.

**TOOLS:** plastic sheeting and tarps; stepladder; paint buckets (one for each color); stirring sticks; paintbrushes (natural bristle for oil-based paint and polyurethane, man-made bristles for latex paint); 4- or 5-inch-wide soft brushes or large sponge; roller with ³⁄₁₆- or ³⁄₈-inch nap cover; roller tray; clean rags.

### PREPARE THE WALL

Success requires clean, smooth walls. If you have minor cracks, use spray-on crack sealer. Fill holes with spackle and sand smooth. Wash the walls or sand lightly. If you have any stains, they may bleed through no matter how many coats of paint you apply, so cover them with stain-killing primer (available in spray cans as well as regular paint).

If you want the woodwork to be painted differently from the walls, carefully cover it with masking tape—it will be difficult to apply the wash along the edge of woodwork. With a roller and brush, apply the base coat. Even though it will be largely covered, it is important to coat the walls completely. Let the base dry completely.

### MIX THE WASH

Make the wash by thinning 1 part latex paint with 5–9 parts water, alkyd paint with 5–9 parts solvent. Or for latex paint, use an acrylic polyurethane product made for the purpose of color washing (typically, you mix 2 parts paint with 1 part water and 1 part acrylic polyurethane). Use flat interior latex for an aged lime-washed look. Use satin or semigloss interior alkyd to produce a glowing effect. Buy the paints in premixed colors, or buy white paint and mix the colors with universal tints. For a more three-dimensional look, use special textured paint.

When applying the wash, use random strokes and work in large areas.

## BRUSH ON THE WASH

Dip the brush in the first wash coat and slap it onto the wall loosely and irregularly. Work in all directions, varying the size and shape of the patches until 60–70 percent of the base coat is covered. Avoid an even look, and dab or blot out any hard edges.

Or come up with a technique of your own. For instance, you can apply wash with a brush using broad semicircular motions. Or use a large sponge.

Let the first wash dry completely (putting a fan in the room will speed this up dramatically). Apply the second wash the same way, overlapping some of the previous brush strokes and some of the exposed base coat. Let it dry and repeat for the third wash coat. For a deeply glowing effect, finish the walls with a coat of matte polyurethane finish.

## OR USE A GRAINING TOOL

Faux finish possibilities are nearly endless (*see pages 18–19 and 56–59*). Here's one that's fun to apply, though it will take some time. It will give you a look that playfully suggests rather than imitates actual wood grain.

Apply a base coat of latex paint. Use a level and tape measure to draw evenly spaced vertical lines, creating sections that are as wide as your graining tool. Cover every other vertical section with low-stick painter's tape (a paint supplier will have this).

Mix alkyd paint with oil-based glazing liquid according to directions to get a thick paint that will stay wet long enough for you to work with it. Brush on the paint to cover one vertical section.

Immediately use the graining tool, starting at the top of the wall and working downward. Press lightly, and rock the tool back and forth as you pull it. Don't lift up or you'll have to start over again. It will take practice before you get the look you want.

Repeat for all the other vertical stripes. Wipe the graining tool between stripes and use a rag to carefully clean up any dripping paint as you go.

After the paint has dried, remove the masking strips. If you like, you can stop here and have alternating stripes of wood grain and smooth wall surface.

Or apply the glaze and paint mixture to the remaining stripes, and use a graining comb. (A graining tool gives the look of wood with wide grain, but a comb imitates wood with narrow grain.) Wiggle the tool as you pull it downward. Wipe away any drips as you work.

Pull the graining tool down and rock it back and forth as you work.

# CHANGE INTO STRIPES

Simple vertical stripes lend an old-fashioned air to walls that busier wallpaper cannot match. The effect is subtle rather than flowery. And because you paint the stripes yourself, you can choose the exact color you want. On these pages we present two striping possibilities. Shadow striping gives a formal, subtle pattern to your walls, while squeegee striping produces a more playful effect. Both techniques are within the reach of a do-it-yourselfer, but they are time-consuming. Expect to spend several days working on an average hallway.

*Perk up a room by painting in stripes of slightly different colors or by simply alternating between flat and glossy versions of the same color.*

## SHADOW STRIPING

This is done by alternating flat stripes with glossy stripes of the same color. The difference will be more noticeable when you look along the length of a wall, which makes this a great technique for a hallway. Smooth the walls and apply a coat or two of flat wall paint. Allow at least a day for the paint to dry completely before applying tape to it.

Choose the width of low-stick painter's tape to suit your taste. Wide stripes look more formal than narrow ones. You can alternate stripes of the same width or have two different widths.

## APPLY THE GLOSSY PAINT

With a level, make faint pencil lines to indicate a plumb line in the middle of the wall. Roll and press a strip of tape from the ceiling to the wall. Working outward from the middle, use small pieces of tape as spacers, to line up the rest of the stripes of tape.

Pour glossy paint into a tray and apply to the untaped portions of the wall with a roller that approximates the width of the stripes. Immediately follow with a paintbrush, working in long strokes and making sure all the gaps are filled.

While the paint is still wet, carefully pull off the tape. Pull straight away from the wall to be certain you do not smear any paint. You definitely need to practice on a wall surface and become confident in your technique before doing the job.

## SQUEEGEE STRIPING

This method requires less in the way of preparation, but you do need a steady hand. Don't expect perfection; a few unsteady lines and a drip here and there will add charm and emphasize that the job was done by hand. Still, work as carefully as possible because too many mistakes will result in a sloppy look.

Smooth the walls and apply a solid coat or two of latex paint for a base coat. The smoother the wall and the glossier the base coat, the more cleanly the squeegee will be able to wipe paint off the surface.

## WHAT YOU'LL NEED

**MATERIALS:** paints; glazing liquid (for squeegee striping); low-stick painter's tape; masking tape.

**TOOLS:** drop cloths; paintbrushes; roller; ladder; level; pencil; squeegee; utility knife; straightedges for squeegee striping.

Wait a day before removing low-stick painter's tape

## MAKE THE STRIPER AND MIX THE PAINT

Purchase a window-washing squeegee about 12 inches wide. Use a sharp utility knife to cut out square notches in the rubber part. You can try for evenly spaced notches or cut out variously sized and spaced notches for more visual interest.

For making stripes, you need paint that will not dry quickly and will respond well to the squeegee. Mix 3 parts glazing liquid with 1 part paint or consult with your paint dealer for a ready-made product. Make enough to do the whole room.

## SET UP THE JOB

Because you must always work in strips that are as wide as your squeegee, you will not be able to maintain the exact pattern throughout the room. When you come to the end of a wall or when you meet an obstruction, such as a window, the pattern will have to be varied. Do this by overlapping squeegee strokes.

Plan the job by measuring the walls and figuring where you will have to overlap squeegee strokes. Try to minimize overlap or put pattern changes in places where they will not be very visible. For instance, on a wall with a window, it may make sense to start at one corner and work toward the window, then start at the other corner and work in the opposite direction until the stripes meet under the window.

Have on hand a long straightedge that reaches from floor to ceiling, as well as a short straightedge for places such as under a window.

## MAKE THE STRIPES

With a roller, apply the glaze/paint mixture to the wall in a vertical stripe as wide as the squeegee. (It helps to have a roller sleeve that is as wide as the squeegee.)

Immediately follow with the squeegee, using a straightedge to keep your lines straight. The straightedge should measure almost the height of the ceiling. Be sure you can keep it still while you work—have a helper hold it in place against the wall. Because walls are rarely perfectly plumb, use a level even when you are starting in a corner.

As you pull the squeegee down from the ceiling to the floor, press firmly enough to remove paint but not so firmly as to make smudges.

After each set of stripes, wipe the squeegee and the straightedge clean. Use the squeegee as a measuring tool to accurately position the straightedge, both top and bottom, for each successive set of stripes. For short spaces, use a short straightedge.

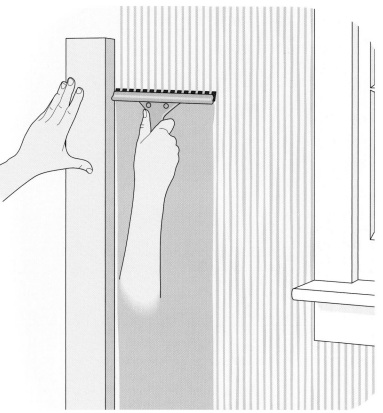

*Hold the squeegee straight and press fairly firmly as you pull down from ceiling to floor.*

# BRIGHTEN WOOD PANELING

Most of the veneered plywood paneling installed in American homes between 1963 and 1977 has a dark wood tone that can seem oppressive. However, you don't need to tear out paneling to get cheery walls. (In some cases, tearing it out would be disastrous because paneling was sometimes installed over studs without wallboard first being hung.) Instead, paint it. The paneling will take on an entirely new look and give the room a textured character, as well as a bright atmosphere. Excellent color choices include white, off-white, ivory, beige, light taupe, pale or bright pastels, and muted or grayed pastels. If the paneling is in decent condition, you can paint an average bedroom in a day.

*Simply painting old paneling suddenly turns a gloomy den into a pleasant family room.*

## INSPECT AND PREPARE THE PANELING

Cracks, holes, and other imperfections will not be erased by paint—in fact, paint may actually highlight flaws. Fill such openings with caulk and immediately wipe with a damp sponge, or use wood filler, sanding the surface after it dries.

Lay plastic sheeting along the paneling baseboard and cover with tarps to make it easy to walk on. Then wash the paneling carefully with commercial wall-washing compound. Rinse with clear water containing ¼ cup white vinegar per gallon. Towel dry. Rubbing in the direction of the wood grain, wipe down the paneling with a deglosser to roughen its surface.

## WHAT YOU'LL NEED

**MATERIALS:** tinted alkyd or alcohol-based primer; latex or alkyd interior paint; caulk or wood filler; wall-washing compound; white vinegar; deglosser; mineral spirits.

**TOOLS:** paintbrushes; rollers; sandpaper; plastic sheeting; tarps; commercial sponge; wash bucket; towels; rags.

## PAINTING TECHNIQUE

Choose a paint color. Ask the paint dealer for an alkyd or alcohol-based primer especially formulated to bond to a glossy surface. Have the primer tinted to 75 percent of your color. Apply two coats of this primer with a brush, letting it dry completely between coats. Fill in any imperfections you notice at this point, and prime those spots. Then brush on a coat of flat, eggshell, satin, or semigloss latex (or alkyd interior paint, if preferred). Allow time for the paint to dry.

# PAINT A FLOOR PATTERN

Opaque paint finish offers a quick, affordable, and attractive way to refurbish a badly stained or worn hardwood floor. It's also a great technique for adding a casual or country look to a floor. Another plus: This simple technique produces a durable floor without completely stripping its existing finish.

## WHAT YOU'LL NEED

**MATERIALS:** latex or alkyd floor paint; oil glazes; wood floor cleaner; mineral spirits; white vinegar; polyurethane finish.

**TOOLS:** towels; electric or pole sander with 100-grit sandpaper; tape measure, pencil; T square or framing square; chalk line; kneepads or kneeling pad; paintbrush; coarse graining comb; rags.

## POSSIBLE DESIGNS

Make the project as basic as painting the floor one color or give it a pattern like a checkerboard scaled to the room's size. Compose a checkerboard of two solid but contrasting colors, one color textured with alternating colored glazes, or one color topped with one color glaze combed in different directions to give the alternating squares contrasting texture. Instructions for a traditional checkerboard floor—which creates the illusion of classic tiles—are given here.

## PAINT AND SEAL

Clean the floor thoroughly, and fill or sand any imperfections. Apply a base coat of floor paint (or porch and floor enamel), taking care to completely cover the surface. Allow it to dry completely.

Lay out the design using the T square or framing square as a guide. Following the instructions for planning a ceramic tile layout (*see page 6*), start the design in the center of the floor. Measure accurately and snap chalk lines to mark the pattern on the floor. To keep the job simple, make the checks 12 inches square.

Paint alternating squares so you can clean up the edges of each square as you work. Use one of the following techniques to achieve the look you want:

■ For solid-colored contrasting checks: Paint alternate squares one color; let dry. Paint the remaining squares in the other color. Clean the edges as you complete each square.

■ For a solid color with contrasting glaze coats: When the paint is dry, mix oil glazes according to the instructions given for antiquing painted paneling (*see page 20*). Experiment until you achieve the color,

transparency, and consistency desired. Ideally, you will have a thin, translucent glaze. Brush the first glaze color on alternating squares. Clean the edges as you complete each square. When the glaze is dry, brush the second glaze color on the remaining squares.

■ For a solid color with a combed one-color glaze coat: Use the same technique for contrasting glaze coats, combing the first set of squares from side to side. Wipe the comb frequently to remove glaze buildup. Let the squares dry, then apply the glaze to the remaining squares, combing from top to bottom for contrast.

When the glaze is dry, give the floor one or two coats of clear polyurethane finish.

*A simple checkerboard design hides defects in a wood floor while keeping the look of wood grain.*

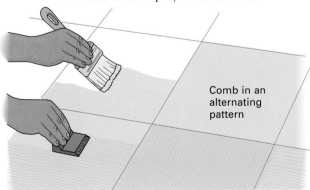

Comb in an alternating pattern

*To achieve a tiled effect, paint, then comb carefully so chalk lines will remain visible.*

# STEP LIVELY ON STENCILS

Here's another technique for producing a handsome floor. If you stencil over an opaque paint, the result playfully imitates an area rug. When the pattern is applied with wood stains on a natural wood floor, it looks like parquetry or inlay. Stenciling also disguises any defects—just incorporate them into the design so they get covered up.

*A stenciled border enhances the beauty of a wood floor while adding the decorative effect of an area rug.*

## CHOOSE OR MAKE A DESIGN

Two rules apply to floor stenciling: Use a simple design with bold, geometric shapes and no more than three colors, and use a separate stencil for each color. Make your own design and cut it out of stencil acetate with a utility knife, or buy a precut design at an arts and crafts supply store. Have the stencils ready and the pattern layout determined before you prepare the floor.

First, draw the layout on graph paper. If the design includes a border, carefully consider its placement. Typical borders run 6–12 inches wide,

## WHAT YOU'LL NEED

**MATERIALS:** spray adhesive or masking tape; stencil paints or wood stains.

**TOOLS:** graph paper; stencil design; stencil acetate; utility knife; cutting board; sandpaper; tape measure; straightedge or T square; pencil; chalk line; kneepads or kneeling pad; stencil brush; small trays for stenciling colors; newspapers; rags; hair dryer; supplies needed for painting a floor (*see page 21*).

depending on the size of the room. Place them either tight to the wall or so that the outside edge is 8 to 18 inches from the wall. The larger the room, the wider you should make the border and the wider the gap you should leave between it and the wall.

## PREPARE THE AREA

Thoroughly clean and lightly sand the floor. If you want to stencil onto a background color, prime and paint the floor. You also can apply stencil paints directly on a floor coated with varnish or polyurethane—clean and lightly sand it first. However, if you want to use wood stains on natural wood, sand away as much of the finish as possible in the areas to be stenciled. If the floor has been waxed, remove the wax.

Measure and snap chalk lines for the design location on the floor. Lay out a border first, starting with the corners, and then evenly space the border design between them. Fill in the field. For an overall design, with or without a border, follow the instructions for planning a ceramic tile layout (*see page 6*). Just as in laying tile, square off the space in each quadrant to accommodate the size of the design.

## STENCILING WITH PAINT

Paint any border corners first, the border design next, and then the field, using the following technique.

■ To stencil with paint, anchor the first stencil in place with spray adhesive or masking tape. Dip the brush into the paint, remove the excess on scraps of newspaper, and apply by pouncing the brush straight up and down against the floor, filling the open area with paint. Don't be surprised if you have to pounce fairly hard with the brush.

■ Carefully remove the stencil. Dry the paint with a hand-held hair dryer. Position the second and third stencils, and paint the colors the same way. Repeat these steps with each section of the design. Clean the stencil and brushes frequently to prevent smearing.

## STENCILING WITH STAIN

To stencil with wood stain, follow the same basic technique for paint but lightly dab the stain through the holes with lint-free rags instead of a stenciling brush. Use only a small amount at a time so the stain doesn't run under the stencil. Repeat as often as necessary to get the desired depth of tone.

When the floor is dry, give it one or two coats of clear polyurethane finish. Use a matte, semigloss, or gloss finish, depending on how much shine you want.

*Trace the desired design onto a sheet of stencil acetate, then tape the sheet to cardboard and carefully cut the stencil with a utility knife.*

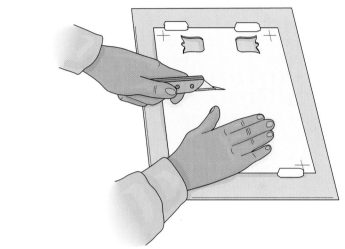

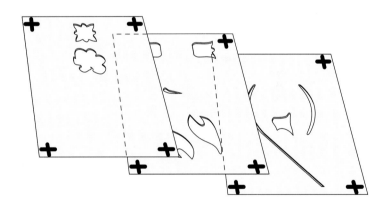

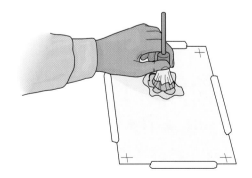

*Plan the stencil with one cutout sheet per color. Add registration marks to line them up. Blot away excess paint on the brush and pounce the brush straight up and down on the stencil. Carefully remove the stencil and clean to avoid smears.*

*No room in the house is harder working than the kitchen, an ideal place for you to add time-saving storage amenities and style upgrades.*

# WORKING ROOMS

All too often, kitchens and bathrooms seem like afterthoughts. They're squeezed into small spaces; they have too little storage room and scant counter space; their lighting is poor; and their fixtures look outdated long before they wear out. Many homeowners assume that the only remedy is high-priced remodeling. Often, however, a few small changes can make a dramatic difference. This chapter offers 17 projects to improve your hard-working rooms without breaking the bank. The ideas range from revitalizing cabinets and appliances inexpensively to solving storage and lighting problems. They prove that no kitchen or bath is beyond redemption.

# PAINT CABINETS, CHANGE HARDWARE

Often, cabinets are discarded only because they show a little surface wear or are the wrong wood tone. However, considering that new cabinets in an average-size kitchen can cost $5,000, it makes sense to look for a less-expensive solution. Paint, plus

**By changing appliances and reworking cabinet doors, you can make a great impact on the appearance of your kitchen without hiring an expensive contractor.**

## WHAT YOU'LL NEED

**MATERIALS:** new door pulls; new hinges; alkyd or latex interior enamel recommended for cabinets; primer/sealer, if needed; commercial wall-washing compound or kitchen degreaser; white vinegar; wood filler; mineral spirits.

**TOOLS:** Drill with screwdriver bit; screwdriver; masking tape; labeling pen; sawhorses or work table; plastic sheets or drop cloths; 200-grit sandpaper; sanding block or power sander; vacuum cleaner; sponge; rags; tack cloth; masking tape; putty knife; fine steel wool; thin-nap paint roller; paintbrushes; paint bucket or tray.

some time and effort, can correct minor deficiencies for 5 percent of that cost or less. Best of all, today's paint products let you skip the messy and exhausting task of removing the existing finish before painting. In fact, don't try to strip the finish—it may be a heat-

cured epoxy that is impossible to remove. For an average-size kitchen with about 25 cabinet doors and drawer fronts, count on spending three or four days preparing, painting, and changing the hardware.

### CHOOSE PAINT AND HARDWARE

Select your paint and new hardware at the same time for a harmonious look. The job will be easier if the door pulls and knobs that you select will fit into the old holes. If not, you will have to fill the holes with wood filler and sand them smooth. Make sure the hinges will work with your doors, as well. (You probably will have to drive screws into new holes.)

Decide what parts of the cabinets you will paint. The easiest solution is to paint only the faces of the frames, the drawer faces, and one side of the doors. But you may prefer to paint both sides of the doors and visible parts of the cabinet interior, too. Shelf bottoms easily can be covered with shelf paper.

Decide whether you like the texture of rolled-on paint or brush strokes. Usually the best solution is to brush the cabinet frame and to roller-paint the doors and drawer faces, using a thin-nap roller sleeve.

### DISMANTLE THE CABINETS

Cover your kitchen or garage floor with plastic sheeting or drop cloths. Lay down a series of long, thin pieces of wood to keep the doors raised as you prepare and paint them.

Dismantling goes quicker if you use a drill equipped with a screwdriver bit. (Most cabinet screws require a No. 1 Phillips-head bit.) Unscrew the hinges and remove the doors. Remove the handles or knobs. Take the drawers off their glides and remove their pulls or knobs. If you plan to reuse hardware, store the pieces so they won't get lost.

### CLEAN AND PREPARE THE WOOD

Airborne grease coats every household surface. It'll ruin the paint job if you don't remove it. Wash the cabinets with a wall-washing compound or kitchen degreaser. Rinse the cabinets with water containing ¼ cup white vinegar per gallon. Wipe them dry and let them air dry for 24 hours. Then wipe them down with mineral spirits to remove all traces of grease. Let them air dry.

Look closely for cracks and other imperfections—they will be magnified by paint rather than covered up. Fill holes with wood filler, let them dry, then sand smooth.

Hold a new hinge in place to see if the screw holes in the doors and frame will line up. If not, fill the holes and sand smooth.

Scuff the cabinets by rubbing sandpaper with the grain just enough to break the surface gloss. Vacuum up the dust and wipe the cabinets with a tack cloth.

## PAINT

Bring a sample door to your paint dealer to make sure your paint will stick. To be absolutely sure, buy an oil- or alcohol-based primer/sealer formulated to block stains and adhere to glossy surfaces. Apply two coats, letting the door dry between coats (about one hour). Buff each coat with fine steel wool. Clean up the dust.

Next, apply two coats of a professional-grade semigloss interior alkyd enamel formulated for painting woodwork. Let the first coat dry 24 hours, then buff with fine steel wool. Clean up the dust before applying the second coat.

Paint the wall cabinets then the base cabinets. Apply each layer of primer/sealer and paint in this order: top trim and rails, bottom rails and underside of wall cabinets, stiles, backside of doors, drawer faces, and drawer fronts and edges.

## REINSTALL WITH NEW HARDWARE

Give the paint plenty of time to dry completely. Even after it is dry to the touch, paint (latex especially) will be soft and easily damaged for a few days. It is best to exercise caution in this case.

If the knobs or pulls fit into the old holes, installing them will be easy—just screw them on. Hinges may be more difficult. If an old hole is too large and the screw doesn't fit tightly, cram a toothpick or other small piece of wood into the hole. If you filled the old holes, drill new ones carefully—don't try to drive screws without pilot holes.

*Ensure that the floor is well covered and the doors are raised up on slats of wood before working on them. Paint the cabinet frames with a brush, and use a roller for the doors and drawer faces.*

# TILE A BACKSPLASH

The area between the top of the countertop and the bottom of the wall cabinets is a magnet for grime that is difficult to wipe off painted walls. Not large enough for hanging pictures, it is often a wide expanse of plain, dull wall surface. Make this space cleaner and brighter by installing wall tiles. If you plan well, you should be able to install the tiles in one day and spend a couple of hours the next day grouting.

Don't be surprised if you spend as much time shopping for tiles as you spend installing them. There are plenty to choose from.

Keep in mind not only the color of the tiles but also the size. Because the area is small (usually about 14 inches from the top of the countertop to the bottom of the cabinet), large tiles may not look good, especially if you have to cut some of them in half. Standard 4-inch-square wall tiles make a good choice. You also can consider buying mosaic tiles—small tiles that come in sheets. These can give a more distinctive appearance.

Most countertops come with their own backsplashes, usually 4–5 inches high. In some cases, it may be possible to remove this and install new tiles all the way down to the top of the counter surface. Usually, however, it is best to leave the backsplash in place.

*Tiling the area between the countertop and the wall cabinets adds charm and makes it easier to keep your kitchen clean.*

## WHAT YOU'LL NEED

**MATERIALS:** tiles (field tiles, caps pieces, and corner tiles if needed); wall tile adhesive (ask dealer for correct type); grout; liquid latex grout additive; grout sealer; mineral spirits; caulk.

**TOOLS:** Tape measure; tile cutter; tile nippers or hacksaw with tile-cutting blade; notched trowel (ask dealer for correct size); laminated grout float; sponge; rags; bucket.

Make a rough drawing of your area and bring it with you to a tile dealer. Wherever you have exposed tile edges, buy special cap pieces—the edge of a regular field tile will look unfinished and be difficult to clean. Wherever there will be a tile with two exposed edges, buy a special corner piece.

Choose grout at the same time as the tiles. It is usually best to avoid grout that contrasts strongly with the color of the tiles because any small imperfection in your installation will be magnified. Ask the dealer to recommend the correct adhesive and notched trowel for your tiles.

## DO A DRY RUN

Make sure you know how the tiles will fit before you start spreading adhesive. Measure the distance from countertop to cabinet bottom in several places to see if some tiles will need to be cut to different sizes.

With a helper or two, hold tiles in place to see how they will look. Usually, you'll want to start with a whole tile at the bottom because the top will not be very visible. Line the tiles up lengthwise and make sure you will not end up with slivers at either end.

## SET THE TILES

Spread the adhesive with a notched trowel, working carefully so that the entire area is covered. Hold the trowel at about a 45-degree angle to the wall so that you end up with ridges of consistent depth. Work in long strokes wherever possible to produce a straight surface. Wipe up any spills with a rag dampened with mineral spirits; keep your hands clean of adhesive.

Set standard tiles by pressing each into place with a slight twist. If you are working with sheets of mosaic tile, hold each sheet fully spread while you set it in place, then gently smooth it out with your hand.

Make straight cuts with a tile cutter. If you need to cut out a notch, use tile nippers or a hacksaw equipped with a tile-cutting blade. If a piece is slightly too big, do not force it into place because that can throw off your joint lines.

Step back and examine your work periodically to see that the lines are consistent and straight. On mosaics especially, you may have to make slight adjustments. Clean any adhesive off the tile surfaces and wait at least a day for the adhesive to set.

## GROUT, WIPE, AND CAULK

Mix the grout according to directions, using latex additive to increase its strength. Holding the grout float nearly flat, push the grout into the joints, working in several directions to make sure all the joints are completely filled. Then tip the float up and wipe away the excess.

Wipe the surface with a damp sponge, periodically cleaning it in a bucket of water. Eye each grout line to make sure it is smooth and consistent. Allow to dry and buff with a dry rag. Caulk the joint between the countertop and the tiles. After a couple of weeks, apply grout sealer.

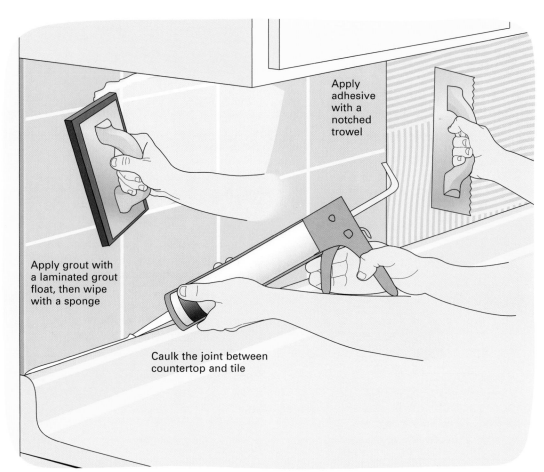

Apply adhesive with a notched trowel

Apply grout with a laminated grout float, then wipe with a sponge

Caulk the joint between countertop and tile

*Once the tile is applied and the grout has cured a few days, seal the junction between tile and countertop with caulk.*

# ADD UNDERCABINET FLUORESCENT LIGHTING

Task lighting does more to make a kitchen a comfortable place in which to work than any other improvement. Without it, you are in your own shadow when you work at a counter. Once lights are installed, you will be pleasantly surprised at how much easier kitchen work becomes.

*This well-lit kitchen combines overhead can lights with cove lighting (on top of the cabinets) and under-cabinet lighting.*

## WHAT YOU'LL NEED

**MATERIALS:** fluorescent fixtures; electrical cable; junction box; twist-on wire connectors; metal cable protectors; electrician's tape; surface-mounted wiring channels and connectors, if installing with cabinets in place; fish tape; electrician's tape.

**TOOLS:** drill; screwdriver; keyhole saw or reciprocating saw; wire strippers; cable stripper; knife; hammer; lineman's pliers.

Fluorescent lighting using standard-voltage wiring makes sense, especially if you are replacing wall cabinets and have the luxury of cutting holes in your walls to run cable. Otherwise, plan on installing surface-mounted wiring, often called raceway wiring. Depending on your situation, the wiring can be difficult, and you may end up with time-consuming wall repairs. If you want to leave your cabinets in place and not cut holes in walls, consider low-voltage halogen lighting (*see page 32*).

Before you begin, check your electrical code requirements. If you have any doubt about your ability to install these lights, hire a licensed electrician to do the job, particularly if you have to run a new circuit from the service panel. Always shut off the power at the service panel before you do any electrical work.

### PLAN LIGHTING FOR THE WHOLE KITCHEN

Poor lighting plagues many kitchens. Correct the problem by coming up with a plan for your entire kitchen. A well-lit kitchen usually has general ceiling lighting, such as recessed can lights (*see pages 14–15*), ceiling lights for highlighted areas, and undercabinet lights.

If your wall cabinets have space above them, consider installing cove lighting. Here, fluorescent fixtures are placed out of sight on top of the wall cabinets, shining up toward the ceiling. Cove lighting produces a dramatic effect. Installing it is easy, since most of the wiring can be simply laid on top of the cabinet.

### RUN THE CABLE

Be sure to shut off the power at the service panel before you begin. Run power to a switch box and then run cable to the individual fluorescent fixtures. Check each fixture to see where the cable will enter it. Plan on a series of fixtures running along the underside of your cabinets, covering about half of the total length of the cabinets.

If the cabinets are removed, run most of the cable in the space that will be covered by the new cabinets. Carefully mark the exact locations of the bottoms of cabinets and avoid making holes that go below the light fixtures. Make notches at the studs and protect cable with metal pieces at each stud. Have the cable poke through the wall at the correct spots for entering the fixtures. Work so as to minimize damage to visible walls—often, wall repair takes longer than the electrical installation.

To install fluorescent fixtures with the cabinets in place, use a surface-mounted (raceway) wiring system. To use it, install the channels and connectors on the wall and/or cabinet, run the wires, and snap on the covers. This allows you to run high-voltage wiring without cutting holes in walls.

## INSTALL THE FIXTURE PLATES

Disassemble each light fixture by removing the plastic light cover and the housing for the wiring. If the lights do not come with cable connectors for clamping the cable as it enters the light, you will have to buy some. (If your lights are only an inch thick, you will need special small connectors.)

Secure the cable connector to the knockout hole in the fixture plate and push

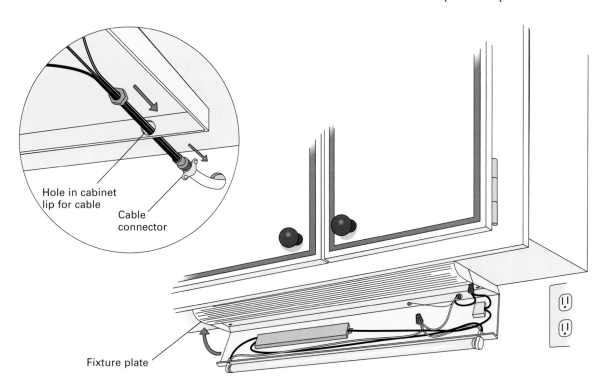

Hole in cabinet lip for cable

Cable connector

Fixture plate

## INSTALL THE CABINETS

If your cabinets have lips at the bottom, cut or drill holes for the cable to run through. (Usually, the light fixture is thicker than the lip and covers it, so you don't have to cut precisely.)

Determine exactly where the fixtures will be attached to the cabinets. Usually, it is best to set the lights as far back as possible so they will not be visible. If a light fixture will span two cabinets that have bottom lips, you will need to notch the lips to accommodate the fixture. Install the cabinets carefully, so as not to damage the cable where it pokes through the wall.

the cable through it. Unless the fixture is at the end of the run, two cables will enter it— one bringing power and one sending power to the next fixture. Be sure there is enough cable in the fixture to allow you to make the connections. Tighten the connector to make the cable secure. Push the fixture plate into place and attach it to the underside of the cabinet. Be sure to use screws that will not poke into the interior of the cabinet.

## MAKE THE CONNECTIONS

Hook up the wiring, connecting black wires to black wires, white to white, and ground to ground. Because these fixtures are thin, you need to plan the locations of splices carefully to ensure that the cover can be reattached.

Install the bulbs, restore power to the wall switch, and test. You may need to adjust the bulbs and starters (if any) to get everything working. Turn off the power and replace the covers on the fixtures. Test again.

# INSTALL HALOGEN UNDERCABINET LIGHTING

How can you brighten your kitchen work spaces without the mess and complications of standard lighting? Halogens supply the answer. Low-voltage lighting means almost no danger while you work. Because the lights are turned on and off with a battery-powered remote-control switch, there is very little wiring to connect. In fact, you connect to power by simply plugging into a handy electrical receptacle.

## WHAT YOU'LL NEED

**MATERIALS:** lights; switch; transformer; power block; wiring (all in a kit).

**TOOLS:** drill; screwdriver; wire strippers; lineman's pliers.

You will end up with exposed wires, but they will not look out of place because they are so thin. To install a system like this with six or seven lights, count on spending most of a day. Near a handy receptacle, drill holes through a cabinet to allow wires to pass through. Run wires from the receiver module into the cabinet. Attach a transformer and power block to the inside of the cabinet and hook up the wires. The wires cannot be cut, so you may have to coil and tape them out of the way.

## ATTACH THE LIGHTS

Disassemble each light and attach the base to the underside of the cabinet. Run the wires along the cabinet so they are not visible. Drill small holes and run the wires into the cabinet, and attach to the power block.

The switch can be installed anywhere. Simply attach the switch housing to the wall or side of a cabinet with screws. Use plastic anchors to attach to drywall. Install a battery and screw the coverplate to the housing.

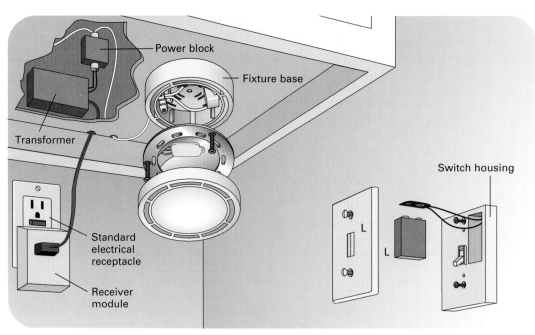

*Halogen lights brighten counter space beautifully and require a minimum of work to install.*

Power block

Fixture base

Transformer

Switch housing

Standard electrical receptacle

Receiver module

# ADD UNDERCABINET ACCESSORIES

Lights aren't the only conveniences that can be hidden under wall cabinets. Use this neglected space to store items that would otherwise take up precious shelf or counter space. Many small appliances—including microwave ovens, coffee makers, toasters, and electric can openers—mount under cabinets. Convenient storage accessories also fit into this space. Look for them at home centers or kitchen-cabinet outlets. Cabinetmakers may sell or custom-make accessories, as well. Below are descriptions of some of the most useful ones.

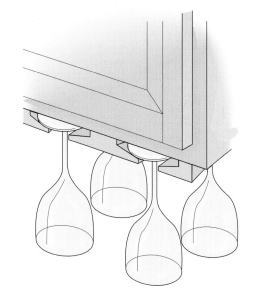

*A wine-glass rack, cup holder, and book holder are just three of the many accessories available for installing under your wall cabinets.*

## WHAT YOU'LL NEED

**MATERIALS:** accessories and accompanying hardware; screws, if needed; stain or paint; wood filler.

**TOOLS:** drill with screwdriver bit; screwdriver; tape measure; saw; sandpaper.

■ This wine-glass rack is made from the same molding that holds glasses within easy reach of a bartender. Locate the rack where you will not bump the glasses. Measure the space under the cabinet and cut the molding strips to length. Mount them with countersunk wood screws driven through pilot holes, placing them just far enough apart to allow the glasses to slide between them. Fill the screw holes; stain and finish or paint.

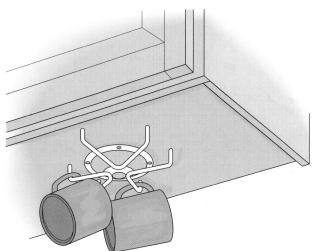

■ Whether revolving or stationary, hanging cup holders give you a handy way to store coffee mugs or cups under a cabinet. They come with the screws needed to mount them.

■ This kind of holder is perfect for a cookbook, knife, or spice racks. When needed, it pulls down and forward on spring-loaded brackets. The fixture comes with the screws and instructions needed for installation.

■ Sometimes the simplest solutions are best. A row of brass or chrome hooks, evenly spaced under a cabinet, can showcase your mug collection or display measuring cups and spoons within easy reach. A simple book rack, made of the same material as your cabinet, can house all your cookbooks. Or a small wine rack can house a dozen or so bottles.

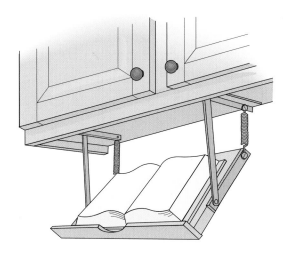

# HANG A POT RACK

Free up cabinet space by adding a handsome hanging rack to store pots, pans and large items like deep kettles. (Store the lids using a handy rack in a base cabinet—*see page 35*.) Buy one at a kitchen-supply source or make one according to the directions below. Hanging or making a rack will take a couple of hours.

## MAKE A RACK

Locate the ceiling joists over the rack area and mark the positions of the ceiling hooks. Measure between them to determine the overall size and shape of the rack, either a square or a rectangle.

Cut four pieces of brick molding to length. Miter the corners and join with wood glue and countersunk wood screws. Fill the screw holes and finish with paint or stain. Drill pilot holes into the top near the corners. Fasten screw hooks into them and attach the chains. Drill pilot holes in the ceiling hook locations. Tighten screw hooks through the ceiling into the joists and hang the rack.

Hook commercial hangers over the rack to support pots and pans. Or drill pilot holes in the bottom edge of the rack and insert additional screw hooks to hang pans.

## HANG A RACK

Locate the joists in the ceiling, using a stud finder. As much as possible, match the locations of the four ceiling hooks with the dimensions of the pot rack so that the chains will hang straight down.

For each ceiling hook, drill a pilot hole. Screw the ceiling hook into the joist by inserting a screwdriver into it sideways and turning until the flange of the hook touches the ceiling. Cut four sections of chain to the same number of links, and attach them to the pot rack. With a helper, lift the rack and hang the chains on the ceiling hooks.

*Count the links in the chain to determine equal lengths. Fasten hooks directly into ceiling joists for greatest support.*

## WHAT YOU'LL NEED

**MATERIALS:** for hanging rack—screw hooks; chains; ceiling hooks; for making rack—brick molding; wood screws; wood filler; stain or paint.

**TOOLS:** for hanging rack—ladder; screwdriver; stud finder; tape measure; pencil; drill; for hanging rack—miter box; wood glue.

# CABINET RACKS

Few kitchens have enough storage space. The practical solution is to organize cabinets so they hold more. Wire storage accessories offer an affordable way to do this. Good home centers, storage-system shops, and cabinet-supply stores sell such accessories. They require minimal installation, if any, and come with good instructions and the necessary hardware. Installing them usually takes less than an hour.

## WHAT YOU'LL NEED

**MATERIALS:** racks and holders with hardware.

**TOOLS:** screwdriver or drill with screwdriver bit; hacksaw; stud finder.

## USE EVERY INCH OF SPACE

A host of practical accessories makes maximum use of unused walls, shelves, door backs, and drawers. They include:
■ Tiered units that store items at different levels on the same shelf.
■ Helper shelves that create two shelf spaces on one shelf.
■ Cup and lid racks.
■ Vertical and stacked plate racks.
■ Vertical dividers that make storage slots for baking sheets and trays.
■ Kitchen-wrap and paper-bag racks.
■ Caddy baskets that create shallow shelves on the back of doors.
   Flat grids equipped with hooks and clip-on baskets quickly turn unused wall space into storage space.

## GRID HOLDERS

These make your kitchen a more pleasant workplace and put often-used items, such as the frying pan or spatulas, within quick reach. Choose a model that can be wiped clean easily, especially if you will be placing it near the cooktop.
   Take your dimensions along when you buy the rack, so a home center or specialty store can cut the holder to fit. If not, cut it yourself with a hacksaw. To install it, locate the studs and drive screws through the clips that hold the grid in place.

## SHELF RACKS

Be specific when choosing these racks. Decide which plates, cups, and other items you want to store, and make the appropriate purchase.
   Sometimes you don't need more space but need to be able to see the items stored in the back of a cabinet. Tiered shelves are great for making spices and other small items visible.

## DOOR RACKS

When measuring for a rack that will attach to the back of a door, make sure it will not bump into the cabinet frame; usually, the rack must be at least several inches narrower than the door. Make sure, too, that the rack will not be so deep that it bumps into shelves. Cabinet doors hang on small hinges and are not designed to hold a lot of weight, so it may be best to choose a small rack.

*Easily installed cabinet and wall organizers include a grid holder, an upright rack for lids or plates, a cup holder, tiered shelves for small items, and a rack that hangs on the back of a door.*

# CABINET SLIDE-OUTS AND DRAWERS

Here are some more ideas for increasing your storage space without going to the expense of adding new cabinets. Though your kitchen may seem crowded, chances are there is plenty of unused space. Most of these items can be installed in an hour or two.

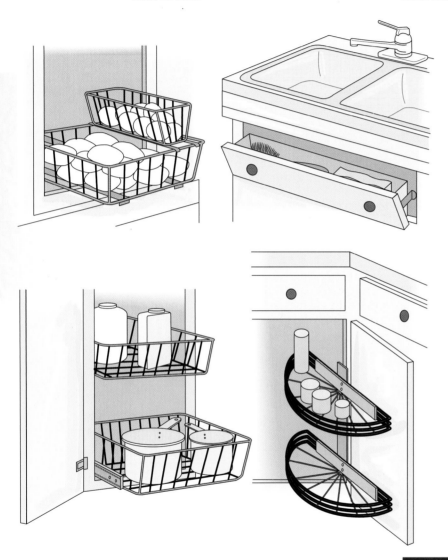

**More ways to make your kitchen better organized and easier to use: roll-out basket shelves of various sizes, a sink-front tray, and half-moon swing-out shelves.**

## WHAT YOU'LL NEED

**MATERIALS:** units and accompanying hardware; screws if needed.

**TOOLS:** drill with screwdriver bit; screwdriver; tape measure; small level.

## ROLL-OUT BASKET SHELVES

Eliminate all that kneeling and searching for what's in the rear of a base cabinet by installing a roll-out unit. They come in a variety of sizes. Many are strong enough to hold heavy pots. Some have lift-out sections you can carry.

There also are roll-out trash-bag holders and undercabinet recycling baskets. Measure the opening before buying one of these units—they come only in certain standard sizes. If no rack is available to fit your opening, you may be able to add wood pieces on one or both sides to accommodate a smaller rack.

The racks slide on two glides. Position each slider so it is level with the other and so the front of the slider reaches the front of the cabinet frame. Make sure each is level and install by driving screws. The most difficult part may be maneuvering into the space to drive the screws.

## SINK-FRONT TRAY

This tray doesn't hold much, but it can be a great help because it can keep sponges and other small cleaning items within easy reach yet out of sight. Measure the false front panel under the sink before buying a tray.

To install one, pry off the false front panel of the sink cabinet. Some panels need to be detached from the inside of the cabinet. Install the hinges on either side with screws. Mount the tray onto the hinges, making sure that the face is in line with the countertop.

## HALF-MOON SWING-OUTS

These shelves let you use the space at the back of blind-corner cabinets. Some attach to the door and swing out when it opens. Others mount on a post assembly installed inside the cabinet; they swing out and slide forward. There also are full-round and pie-cut carousel shelf units for full corner cabinets. Measure openings and cabinet spaces carefully and bring the figures to a dealer before choosing which unit is best for you.

# REPAIR A DRAWER

A drawer that sticks or doesn't close all the way can become annoying. If you leave it that way, further damage is likely to result as the drawer gets twisted and forced every day. But there's no reason to live with this situation. For a modest investment and an hour or two of your time, you can get that drawer gliding smoothly again.

## WHAT YOU'LL NEED

**MATERIALS:** set of glides with accompanying hardware; wood glue; small screws or nails.

**TOOLS:** drill; screwdriver; hammer; clamps; small square; small level.

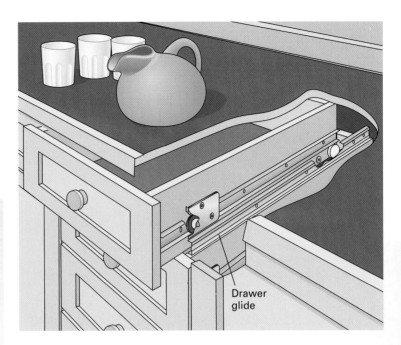

Drawer glide

## INSPECT THE DRAWER AND OLD HARDWARE

Pull the drawer all the way out of the cabinet. Some models simply pull out, some need to be lifted upward at the end, and others have hardware on the sides that must be flipped up before the drawer will come out.

Take a look at the drawer. It should be solid and free of deep scratches. If it wobbles, reinforce it by drilling pilot holes and driving small screws or nails. Or apply wood glue and clamp firmly for 24 hours. In either case, use a small square to make sure the drawer is perfectly square as you work.

Examine the hardware. Older types may have a central runner and plastic rollers on either side or a similar arrangement. You may be able to reattach the parts to get the drawer moving again. For a more permanent fix, install new hardware as shown below.

## INSTALL NEW SLIDING HARDWARE

This type of drawer hardware costs more than others, but it is easy to install, allows the smoothest glide, and will last for a long time.

You may need to add strips of wood to the side of the cabinet in order to have a surface for attaching the glides, but most cabinets will accept them readily. Use a small shim to raise the piece slightly above the cabinet frame. Attach the front end by drilling pilot holes and driving screws. Check for level and attach the rear end.

The other part of the glide attaches to the side of the drawer. Position it so that the front touches the back of the drawer face and the flange on the other end sits under the bottom of the drawer. Attach the back with screws, check to ensure the glide is parallel with the bottom of the drawer, and attach the front with screws.

*You don't have to be a professional to install new hardware that makes a drawer slide straight and smoothly.*

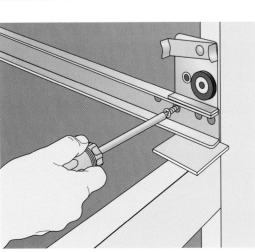

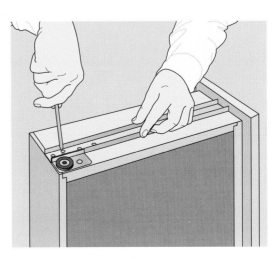

# BUILT-IN IRONING CENTER

Save yourself the awkwardness of lugging an ironing board around the house by installing a built-in ironing center between the studs in a utility room or kitchen wall. Equipped with drop-down board, electrical outlet, timer, light, clothes hook, and storage shelf, this ready-to-install cabinet makes a bothersome chore much easier.

Installing the cabinet will take about half a day, but providing electrical service may take a while, especially if you need to add a new circuit.

Before you begin, check local electrical code requirements. If you have any doubt about your ability to wire the center, hire a licensed electrician to do the job.

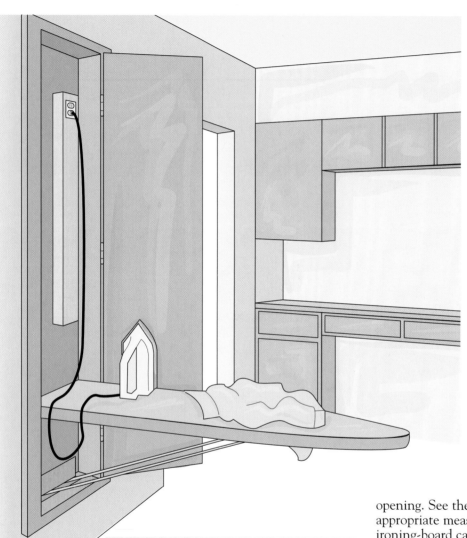

*An ironing center allows you to quickly hide or pull out an ironing board.*

## WHAT YOU'LL NEED

**MATERIALS:** built-in ironing center; 2×4s; 1×4, if needed; 10d nails; shims; No. 12 1½-inch screws; electrical junction box; 15-amp circuit breaker, if needed; electrical cable; twist-type wire connectors, electrical tape, cable connectors; cove molding; finishing nails; wood filler; stain or paint.

**TOOLS:** stud finder; tape measure; pencil; carpenter's level; keyhole or reciprocating saw; hammer; nail set; lineman's pliers; wire stripper.

### PLAN THE LOCATION

Designed for recessed mounting, the cabinet requires an opening measuring 14¼ inches wide and about 48 inches high. The wall must be a standard 4½ inches thick or thicker. You need at least 16 inches of wall space on one side of the opening to accommodate the door's swing and 47 inches of open floor space in front to accommodate the open ironing board. When closed, the cabinet projects 2½ inches into the room.

Decide how high above the floor the ironing board should stand; this determines how high above the floor to start the opening. See the manufacturer's chart for the appropriate measurement for your specific ironing-board cabinet.

### CUT THE OPENING

The ironing unit must be installed between two wall studs that have a 14½-inch space between them. Use a stud finder to locate studs, or use a hammer and nail, taking care not to make test holes outside the area where the unit will go.

Once the studs have been located, lightly draw the outline of the cutout on the wall. Use a keyhole saw or reciprocating saw to cut it out. You will actually use the studs as guides, holding the saw blade against them as you cut, to make straight vertical cuts. Do not saw too deeply, or you may poke a hole in the other side of the wall.

## INSTALL THE ELECTRICAL SERVICE

Check the label on your iron to see how many amps it pulls. You may be able to grab power from an existing kitchen circuit, as long as doing so will not cause you to overload the circuit. Or it may be necessary to install a new 15-amp circuit. Consult an electrician if you are unsure about this step.

Shut off the power at the service panel. Fish cable from a nearby lighting outlet, receptacle, or new circuit into the ironing center opening. If you need to run cable across studs, cut notches and install protective metal plates wherever there is danger of hitting the cable with a nail. Leave 2 feet or so of extra cable hanging out to make sure you have enough to work with when you install the cabinet.

## INSTALL THE CABINET

Cut short pieces of 2×4 blocking to fit horizontally between the studs, and install one at the top and one at the bottom of the opening. Check the size of the opening and make adjustments by adding a 1×4 piece, if necessary.

The ironing cabinet has at least one knockout hole for the electrical service. Punch one out and install a cable clamp. Pull the cable into the cabinet and tighten the clamp to secure the cable. Set the cabinet in the opening, then plumb and shim to fit. Use a small square to see that it is not out of square; otherwise, the unit may not operate smoothly.

Starting a foot from the top, drill pilot holes every 2 feet or so along the sides and bottom of the cabinet frame. Drive screws through the frame into the studs. Test the ironing board and make adjustments, if needed, by shimming.

Strip the cable sheathing then the ends of the wires. Connect the wires to the pigtails in the bottom of the wireway of the ironing center and install the cover. Restore power and test the receptacles.

Trim around the center with cove molding, mitering the corners and driving finishing nails. Set the nails and fill the holes. Repair the wall where you ran the cable. Stain and apply a clear finish, or prime and paint.

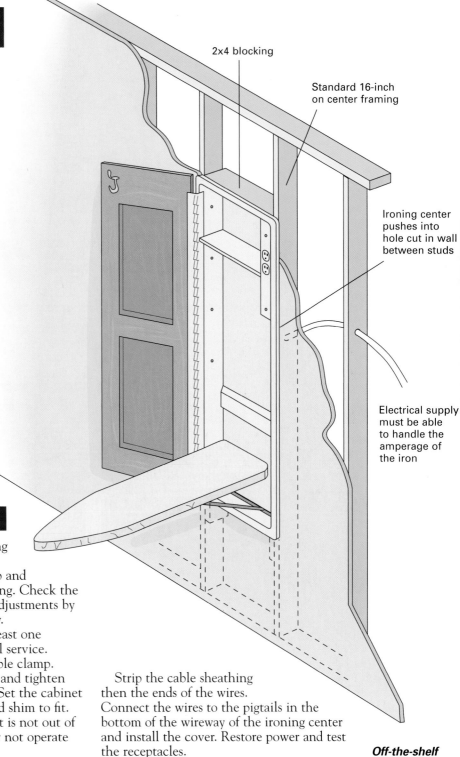

2x4 blocking

Standard 16-inch on center framing

Ironing center pushes into hole cut in wall between studs

Electrical supply must be able to handle the amperage of the iron

*Off-the-shelf units are designed to fit between the studs of a wall.*

# ADD A CABINET-END BOOK RACK

**P**ut the exposed ends of kitchen cabinets to work with this simple cookbook holder. It's sized to fit the end of any base cabinet, particularly on a peninsula or island. Build two and place them 15 inches apart, securing them to the cabinet with wood screws. If you like, you also can make the holder 12 inches narrower to fit the end of a wall cabinet.

Take the end-piece pattern (*below right*) to a copy center, and enlarge it until it is full scale. Use it to trace and cut one end piece with a saber saw; sand it smooth. Use the first end piece as the pattern for the other one.

Cut the shelf out of 1×4 and the two slats out of 1×2. Measure accurately and drill pilot holes in each piece as shown in the illustration below. Be sure to align the pilot holes in adjoining pieces.

Apply glue to the shelf ends and screw the end pieces to them. Apply glue to the front edges of the end pieces and screw the 1×2 slats across the front, aligning them so they are parallel. Sand the holder lightly. Clean up the sanding dust. Fill the screw holes and let dry. Sand over the filled holes until level. Clean up the dust. Stain and apply polyurethane finish, or prime and paint; allow the shelf to dry completely before installing.

Set the holder against the cabinet, with the bottom of the end pieces 13 inches below the bottom edge of the countertop. (Increase this distance if you have very tall books.) Mark the position of the holder on the frame by scoring through the pilot holes with a nail or screw. Set the holder aside. At the scoring marks, drill pilot holes at a 45-degree angle. Reposition the holder and drive screws through the pilot holes into the cabinet frame. If adding a second holder, place it so that the bottom edges of the end pieces are 15 inches below the bottom edges of the first holder. Fill the screw holes. Let dry. Sand and touch up with stain and clear finish, or paint.

*Another way to use every inch of kitchen space: Add a book rack or two to the end of a cabinet.*

## WHAT YOU'LL NEED

**MATERIALS:** 1×4s; 1×2s; 14 1-inch wood screws; four 4-inch wood screws; wood glue; wood filler; wood stain and polyurethane finish, or primer and paint.

**TOOLS:** saber saw; tape measure; pencil; framing square; jigsaw; drill; 3/16-inch drill bit; screwdriver bit; 220-grit sandpaper; sanding block; putty knife; paintbrushes.

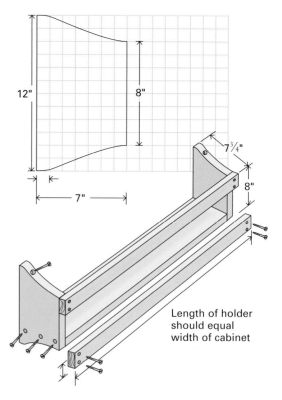

12"   8"   7"   7¾"   8"

Length of holder should equal width of cabinet

# ROMANTICIZE A CLAW-FOOT TUB

If you have an old stand-alone tub that looks dingy, don't assume that you must have a new shower or bathtub installed in order to improve your bathroom. By dressing the tub up with paint, adding a new shower/circular rod unit, and purchasing an attractive curtain, you can save money—and give your bathroom a distinctive touch. The entire project will take a day or two, depending on the condition of your tub.

## PAINT THE TUB

If the inside of your tub is scratched or heavily stained, buy a two-part epoxy enamel made for finishing tubs. Clean and lightly sand the tub. Wipe away the sanding debris and allow the tub to dry completely. Apply the paint. (*See pages 46–47 for detailed instructions.*)

If the claw feet are rusty, take them off, if possible (support the tub with pieces of lumber before removing them). Or work on them in place if you cannot. Scrape off most of the rust with a wire brush. Spray on some rusty-metal primer. Clean and sand the outside of the tub, then paint the feet and the outside of the tub.

## INSTALL FAUCET, ROD, AND SHOWERHEAD

Shut off the water supply. Remove the faucet and take it to a dealer. Purchase a unit that includes tub spout, showerhead, curtain rod, and rods for attaching to ceiling and floor.

Hook up the faucet, using Teflon tape for all the connections. Next comes the pipe with the showerhead. Using a hacksaw, cut the rod securing the shower pole to the wall so that the pole will be plumb and parallel to the wall. Attach the flange to the rod and the rod to the pipe, then attach the bottom of the pipe to the tub faucet. Secure the rod to the wall with screws driven into studs. Or use plastic anchors if you do not hit a stud.

If possible, enlist a helper for installing the circular shower curtain rod. Hold it in place,

check for level, and measure for cutting the rod that extends up to the ceiling. Cut the rod and fasten the flange to its top end. Screw the bottom end into the curtain rod and attach the flange to the ceiling with screws.

You will need two curtains. An all-cloth curtain is often preferred over one with a plastic liner because it won't mildew as easily.

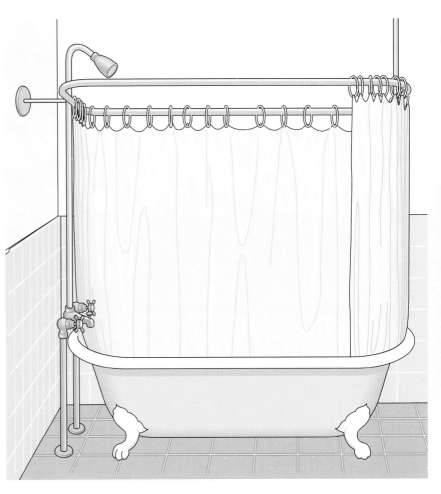

*An old-fashioned tub with shower surround lends charm to a bathroom and saves the cost of installing a new tub or shower.*

## WHAT YOU'LL NEED

**MATERIALS:** two-part epoxy enamel; alkyd- or alcohol-based primer; paint for outside of tub; rusty-metal primer; shower-and-circular-rod assembly with accompanying hardware; Teflon tape; TSP or other heavy-duty cleaner.

**TOOLS:** channel-type pliers; pipe wrench; drill; screwdriver; tape measure; sanding block; 120-grit sandpaper; level; paintbrushes; wire brush; hacksaw.

# FIT BATHROOM SHELVES BETWEEN STUDS

Most baths, like most kitchens, don't have enough storage space. Because they are so small—80 percent of the nation's baths measure 7×9 feet or less—you need to be creative to add storage room.

One solution is to install a new shelf. In most cases, the shelf will have to be less than 4 inches deep (though some plumbing walls are extra thick, allowing for a deeper shelf). But many bathroom items can be stored on 1×4 shelves. Building and finishing a unit like this one will take a day or two.

## CUT A HOLE AND FRAME IT

Purchase a cabinet door and make an opening 1¾ inches larger in both directions than the door.

Tuck shallow, open shelves between the studs on an unused interior wall. Place the opening so a stud forms a jamb on each side. Use a stud finder to locate studs. Or drive a series of test holes with a hammer and nail, starting in the center of the opening to avoid damaging any wall area that won't be cut out. Mark for the opening, using a level and pencil.

Many bathrooms have a special "plumbing wall" (the wall into which the drain pipes disappear). Sometimes this wall is thicker than regular walls, and it may allow you to install deeper shelves. However, beware. There may be pipes running horizontally through the wall, making it impossible to install a cabinet. You often can check a plumbing wall by going to the other side of it and looking for an access panel. If you have one, look into it with a flashlight.

Beware of other possible obstructions. If you have forced-air heat, the space above a head register may be filled with metal duct work. Electrical cable runs through many walls; cut carefully and stop when you feel anything tugging at your saw because it might be a cable. Sometimes the cable is loose enough so that you can loop it around your shelves. If it is not loose, you may need to shut off the power and rerun cable. Consult an electrician if you are not completely sure of your knowledge and skills.

Cut the opening with a keyhole or saber saw, using the inside edges of the studs as guides for cutting straight vertical lines. Be sure not to cut too deeply, or you may poke a hole in the other side of the wall. If you need a wider opening than the usual 14½ inches between studs, carefully cut a stud at two places, 3 inches longer than the rough opening (to make room for 2×4 horizontal pieces at the top and bottom).

Cut two 2×4s to fit between the studs. At the top and bottom of the opening, slip them into the wall and attach them to the studs with angle-driven screws.

*A shallow shelf system like this one is an ideal place for toiletries and cleaning products.*

## WHAT YOU'LL NEED

**MATERIALS:** shelf unit for 14½-inch-wide opening, or 1×6s, 1×4s, and shelf hardware if making shelves; molding for trimming unit; bifold door; hinges; 2-inch screws; finishing nails; plywood and shims, if needed; wood filler; paint or stain with a polyurethane finish.

**TOOLS:** stud finder; tape measure; level; pencil; keyhole or saber saw; hammer; utility knife; miter box with saw; chisel; putty knife; paintbrush.

## BUILD A UNIT

To save time, purchase a ready-made shelf that will fit into your opening. Be sure it is not only the right width and height but also the correct depth. If you do not mind a cabinet that protrudes into the bathroom, buy a deeper unit and trim it around the sides.

To build your own cabinet, first decide whether the rear wallboard looks good enough to act as a back for the cabinet. If not, cut a piece of plywood to fit snugly into the opening.

Rip-cut 1×6 lumber to the correct width so the front edge will be flush with the face of your bathroom wall. You can ask a lumberyard to do this for you.

Cut two pieces to the height of the opening, minus ⅛ inch to make sure these pieces will fit. Cut two pieces to the width of the opening, minus 1⅝ inches (1½ inches to accommodate the thickness of the two 1×4 vertical pieces and ⅛ inch to make sure it fits).

Assemble the four pieces on a flat working surface. Drill pilot holes near the ends of the vertical pieces and drive 2-inch screws, two per joint, through the verticals and into the horizontals. Check to see that the corners remain square as you work.

Install metal shelf standards, two on each of the vertical pieces. Be sure they all are at the same height and check to see that they all face the same direction (it's easy to get one upside down). Fasten with the short screws that come with the standards.

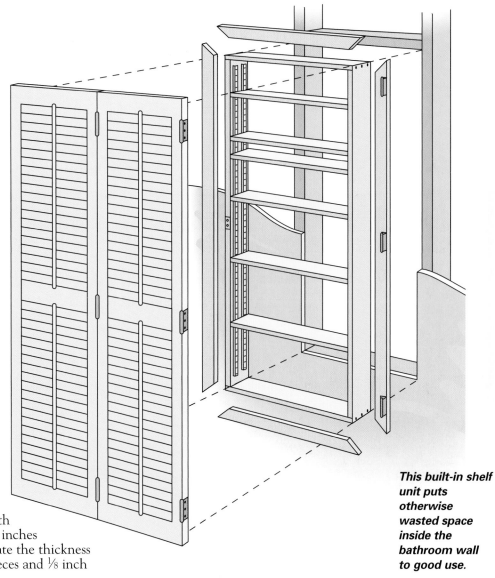

*This built-in shelf unit puts otherwise wasted space inside the bathroom wall to good use.*

## ADD DOORS AND TRIM

Use small shims to position the bifold door so it is centered inside the frame. Mark the hinge positions with a utility knife. Either install the hinges right on the door and the frame, or use the knife and a chisel to cut mortises—precise, shallow cutouts—to accommodate the hinges. Drill pilot holes and attach the hinges with screws.

Purchase molding of your choice—ranch casing for a simple look or colonial casing for a more old-fashioned appearance. Miter-cut the corners and install with finishing nails so that the molding covers about half of the front edge of the cabinet frame.

Paint or stain the cabinet and door. Apply plenty of finish because bathrooms are usually very humid.

# INSTALL A MEDICINE CABINET

Your family spends a good deal of time staring at a mirrored medicine cabinet, so it makes sense to have one that is attractive and useful. Depending on the lighting in your bathroom, you may want to add lights either at the top or on the sides. And if you find that you have to stretch electrical cords across the bathroom, you may want to choose a model that comes equipped with a GFCI (ground fault circuit interrupter) receptacle. Installing a simple cabinet will take a few hours at most; adding electrical service and lights can take much longer. If you are not sure of your electrical knowledge and skills, consult with or hire an electrician.

## FLUSH-MOUNTED OR RECESSED?

A flush-mounted cabinet simply mounts to the surface of the wall; putting one in is a snap. However, it probably will be shallower than a recessed cabinet, and it will protrude into the bathroom space.

If your bathroom does not have a recessed cabinet, there most likely is a reason. Chances are, plumbing pipes lie directly behind the space, making it impossible to fully recess a medicine cabinet. You may want to settle for a flush-mounted cabinet.

But if every inch of space matters and you want a deeper cabinet, it may be worth your while to open up the wall and investigate whether you can at least partially recess the cabinet. Then you can trim it with molding to give it a finished appearance.

## REMOVE THE OLD CABINET

If the old cabinet has electrical lights or a receptacle, shut off the power at the service panel before proceeding. Remove light bulbs and electrical cover plates. Disconnect wires and loosen cable clamps so that the cable can slide freely through the holes.

Empty the cabinet and look for screws or nails holding the cabinet in place. Unscrew or pry out the fasteners, and lift out the cabinet. Avoid damaging electrical cables as you work.

Measure the rough opening and look for a cabinet that will fit. In the case of old houses, you may need to enlarge the opening (a messy business) or close it up some. If the flange of the new cabinet does not cover the opening completely, you will need to install molding.

## CUT AND FRAME A NEW OPENING

Use a stud finder or a hammer and nail to locate the studs. If possible, position the cabinet between studs; otherwise, you will have to cut a notch in a stud to make room for the cabinet.

Draw the rough opening of the cabinet on the wall, checking to see that it is level and

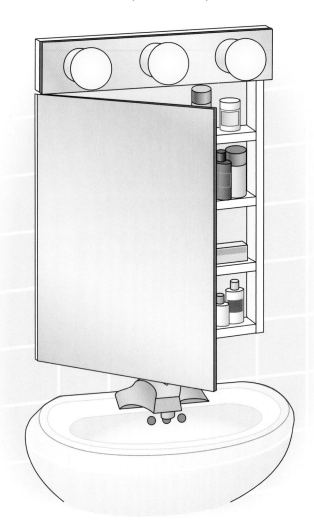

*An attractive light strip above this mirrored medicine cabinet makes it a pleasant place to start the day.*

## WHAT YOU'LL NEED

**MATERIALS:** medicine cabinet; shims and trim molding, if needed; also cable connectors, electrical cable, junction box, twist-on wire connectors, and electrician's tape, if installing lights.

**TOOLS:** drill; stud finder; screwdriver; level; keyhole saw or saber saw; chisel; tape measure; level; framing square; pencil; also lineman's pliers, utility knife, and wire strippers, if installing lights.

square. It should be centered over the sink and at a height that will make the mirror usable by all members of your family.

Work carefully to avoid cutting through any pipes or electrical cables hidden inside the wall. Blueprints may show you where the pipes are. If there is a plumbing access panel on the other side of the wall, open it and look around with a flashlight. Cut slowly, feeling for anything that might be a cable or pipe. Though a keyhole saw is slower than a saber saw, it is safer. Notch studs as needed. If electrical cable needs to be moved, shut off the power at the service panel before touching it.

## RUN ELECTRICAL SERVICE

Shut off the power at the service panel. Run power to the switch then to the opening. If you will be installing lights only, there's no need to worry about overloading a circuit. However, appliances like hair dryers can require plenty of amperage; so if you are installing a receptacle, make sure that the circuit does not service other heavy-amperage appliances or outlets.

Wire connections must be inside a junction box installed in the wall (as shown) or inside the box that is part of the cabinet. Strip the cable sheathing and the tips of the wire ends. Connect to the wires for the light (black wire to black wire, white to white, and ground to ground). Replace the cover plate and secure the cable.

## INSTALL THE CABINET

This is usually a simple task. Slide the cabinet into place and check that it is level and plumb. Make sure the door does not open or close by itself; you may have to shim out the bottom or the top if it does. Attach the cabinet to studs or other framing pieces by driving screws.

## TRIM OUT A PARTIALLY RECESSED CABINET

If you can't slide the cabinet in all the way because of an obstruction in the wall, slide it in as far as you can and attach to the studs with screws. Wrap the perimeter of the cabinet with molding to cover the gap between wall and cabinet. If the side of the cabinet is unattractive, wrap it with molding.

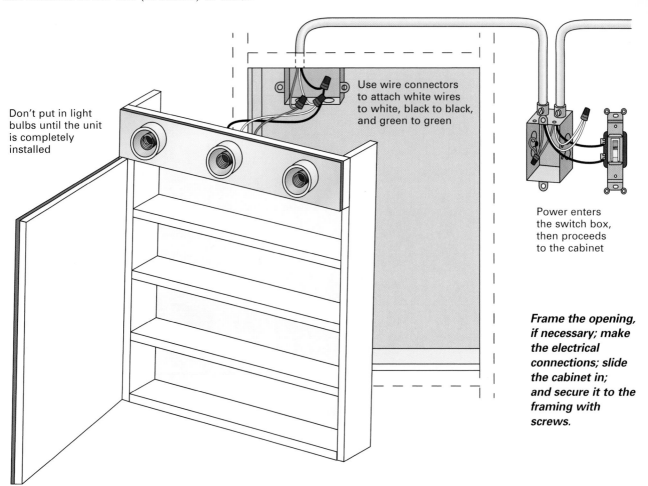

Don't put in light bulbs until the unit is completely installed

Use wire connectors to attach white wires to white, black to black, and green to green

Power enters the switch box, then proceeds to the cabinet

*Frame the opening, if necessary; make the electrical connections; slide the cabinet in; and secure it to the framing with screws.*

# REFINISH A TUB

If your tub has surface cracks or places where the enamel finish has eroded, or if it is stained or just plain dingy, a brand-new tub may seem the only solution. However, if your plumbing is otherwise sound, consider refinishing the tub yourself. This method will not make the tub as good as new but will make it look a whole lot better at a much lower cost than purchasing a new tub and hiring a plumber to install it. (Keep in mind that in many homes the tub was installed *before* the bathroom walls; therefore, you may have to cut through a wall to replace it.) Refinishing a tub yourself doesn't take particular skills, just patience and careful work. Count on spending most of a day preparing and painting the tub. In addition, the refinished tub requires several days to dry and cure before you can use it.

*Give your tub years of new life and a fresh look by refinishing it yourself.*

## REFINISHING OPTIONS

There are plenty of professional tub refinishers. If you hire someone who uses a urethane rather than an epoxy finish, you will end up with better results than you can achieve yourself. Urethane maintains its color better than epoxy and is almost certain not to crack. A good company will apply three coats; you will have to wait three days before using the tub. Make sure the company has been in business for a while and can back up its guarantee.

But a good refinishing job costs plenty of money. Although the result will be better than a do-it-yourself effort, you still will have a refinished tub. You must be careful not to scratch it, and the surface will not look quite as good as that of a brand-new tub. Before hiring a professional refinisher, check with a plumber for the price of a new tub. It may not cost much more than refinishing. Keep in mind that you may have to repair your walls, too; a new tub may be the best solution if you were thinking of changing your tiles anyway.

## WHAT YOU'LL NEED

**MATERIALS:** two-part epoxy enamel; trisodium phosphate or other heavy-duty cleaner; rags; masking tape; auto body filler, if needed.

**TOOLS:** drop cloth; sanding block; 100- and 220-grit sandpaper; natural bristle paintbrush; putty knife.

## CLEAN AND PREPARE THE TUB

It is important to do this carefully, or the epoxy may bubble or flake in time. Thoroughly clean the tub with a strong cleaner. Use sandpaper to smooth any high spots and rough up the entire inner surface of the tub. First go over it with medium-grit paper, then use fine paper.

If the tub has any chipped-out areas or indentations, mix a small amount of auto body filler, apply it with a putty knife, allow it to dry, and sand perfectly smooth.

Carefully cover the walls next to the tub with masking tape. If there is a spout or handle in danger of getting spattered with enamel, remove or cover it completely with masking tape.

Wipe away all dust with a clean, dry rag and take steps to ensure that no dust enters the bathroom. Wait at least overnight for the tub to become absolutely dry.

## MIX AND PAINT

Open the cans of the two-part epoxy, and thoroughly mix as much as you will need. Brush on the epoxy, using a high-quality bristle brush that is not likely to lose bristles as you work.

Painting epoxy is a bit tricky. Move the brush in one direction only instead of back and forth. Cover each area completely before moving on and go over the surface only once; if you go back over a spot a minute or so later, the paint may peel away or you may end up with an unsightly ripple.

Allow the paint to dry for a day, then repaint. Once you have finished, peel the masking tape away. Keep the area dust free for several days before using the tub.

## ORDER A TUB INSERT

Here's another solution: You can find a company that specializes in making fiberglass or high-gloss acrylic inserts that fit into your tub. Hundreds of sizes and styles are available. The company will measure your tub, then return several weeks later with an insert. The insert is permanently glued to the old tub, giving you a surface that is superior to a refinished tub. This process, however, costs more than refinishing.

*To refinish a tub, begin by patching any chips in the enamel and sanding the surface before applying the tub refinishing paint.*

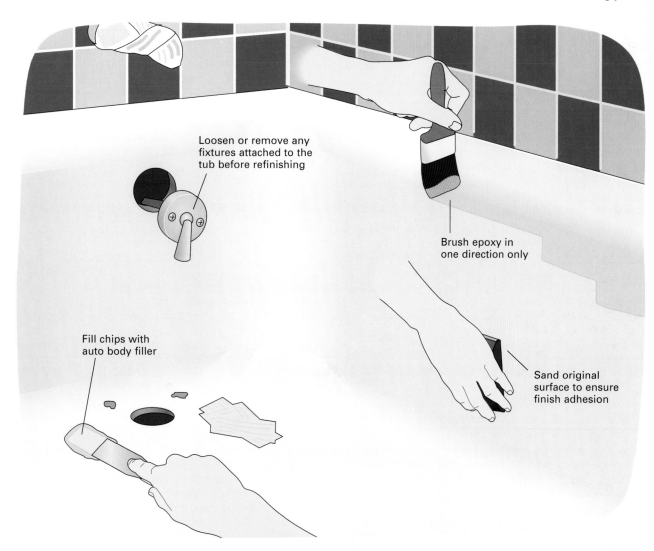

Loosen or remove any fixtures attached to the tub before refinishing

Brush epoxy in one direction only

Fill chips with auto body filler

Sand original surface to ensure finish adhesion

# REPLACE A FAUCET

Nothing gives away the age and condition of a home more quickly than its plumbing fixtures. Why not replace them? Faucets come in many styles; most are designed for do-it-yourself installation and come with easy-to-follow instructions. Just be sure the faucet is sized for the fitting holes of the sink.

*A new faucet quickly upgrades a bathroom or kitchen. It can be easier to install than you might expect.*

## REMOVE THE OLD FAUCET

Removing old faucets may be the most difficult part of the job. Clean everything out from under the sink and put a temporary light in the area. If you need more work room, disconnect the P-trap, draining its contents into a bucket. Set a towel in the area to make it more comfortable.

For a bathroom sink with a pop-up drain assembly, disconnect the pop-up rod by loosening the thumbscrew on the clevis (*see page 49*). Slide the rod up and out.

Turn off the angle stops of the faucet. If there are no stops, you need to shut off water to the whole house and drain the line by running a faucet on a lower floor until the water stops. Place a bucket under one angle stop. With a crescent wrench or pliers, loosen the nuts that join the water supply line (also called a riser) to the stop and the faucet. If the space is tight (it often is), a basin wrench is essential. Remove the supply line. Repeat with the other angle stop. Then remove the mounting locknuts that secure the faucet to the sink. Here, again, a basin wrench comes in handy.

Climb out from under the sink. Gently rock the faucet to break its contact with the sink and thoroughly clean the sink deck.

## SECURE THE FAUCET

Place the gasket on the bottom of the faucet escutcheon. If a gasket isn't provided, use plumber's putty. Set the new faucet in place. To secure it to the sink deck, use a basin wrench to screw on and tighten each locknut and washer or spacer on the underbody. A center-set faucet, in which the spout and handle are one unit, may require a single large locknut and washer over the hot and cold water supply tubes and connectors before it can be screwed to the faucet underbody. Follow the manufacturer's

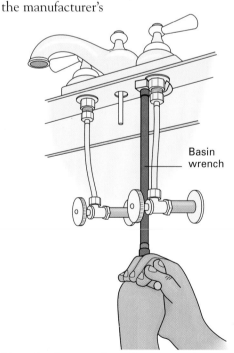

Basin wrench

*Use a basin wrench to disconnect the supply lines at the faucet and to loosen the nuts holding the faucet in place.*

## WHAT YOU'LL NEED

**MATERIALS:** faucet assembly with accompanying hardware; supply lines and connectors, if needed (*see page 49*); Teflon tape; plumber's putty.

**TOOLS:** channel-type pliers; adjustable wrench; pipe wrench; basin wrench; screwdriver; tube cutter; hacksaw.

directions. Either way, fastening the faucet to the deck is easier if someone holds it in place while you work.

## CONNECT THE SUPPLIES

Connect the faucets and their angle stops with their water supply tubes by gently shaping the tubes to align with the two parts. Choose from three types: copper supply tubing; chrome-plated corrugated-copper supply tubing, which is slightly more flexible than copper; or vinyl or stainless-steel-braided flexible water connectors. Each type is sized by its outside diameter (often labeled as "O.D.").

Flexible tubing is sold in precut lengths so it doesn't require cutting or bending. It comes with a captive compression nut and supply nut, so it installs without additional washers, rings, inserts, or sleeves. This means it screws right onto the adapter and angle stop of a faucet and does not require Teflon tape. Consider your options carefully, and don't cut the tubes until you've shaped them and are confident they will align properly.

If required, tightly wrap the faucet end of the tubing several times with Teflon tape. Insert the tube in one of three types of connectors.

■ **BULL-NOSE FLEXIBLE TUBES:** Slip the provided coupling nut onto the tube. Push the top end partway into the faucet's adapter and tighten the nut. Work carefully so you don't strip the threads.

■ **SLIP-JOINT CONNECTION:** This is the ideal connector for copper tubes. Be sure to use the size washer specified by the faucet manufacturer. Slip the coupling nut, washer, and rubber gasket onto the tube, insert the tube in the adapter, and tighten the nut. Work carefully so you don't strip the threads.

■ **FLEXIBLE COPPER INLETS:** If your faucet has these, be careful not to kink them while you work, or the faucet will be ruined. Use two wrenches, one to keep the copper line from twisting and the other to tighten the supply line.

Finish by cutting the tube to the proper length, if necessary, and by pushing the bottom end all the way into the angle stop. Tighten the compression nut and ferrule.

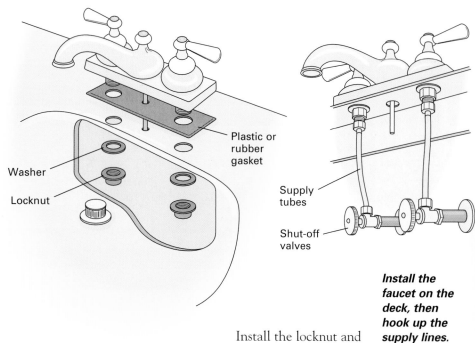

Install the faucet on the deck, then hook up the supply lines.

Install the locknut and holder for the sprayer in the correct hole in the sink's deck. Thread the hose down through the holder and attach to the sink's underbody and faucet, following the manufacturer's directions.

Turn on the water. Remove the aerator and turn on the faucet. Let the lines flush for one minute. Then turn the faucet off and replace the aerator.

## POP-UP DRAIN

Slide the rod through the opening in the faucet, and slip it through the holes in the clevis strap. Tighten the thumbscrew on the clevis strap and test. The stopper should seal when the rod is pulled up. Adjust if necessary.

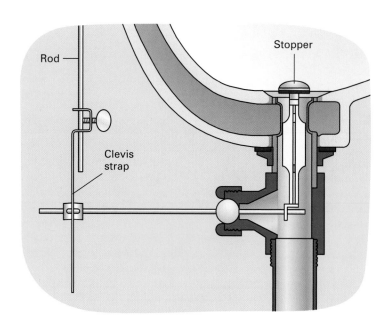

# INSTALL A NEW VANITY

A vanity provides handy storage space for large containers below the sink. It also adds a bit of cabinetry to your bathroom. Surprisingly, a vanity is actually the easiest type of sink to install. The cabinet will cover all the plumbing. Count on spending a day to remove a wall-hung sink and to replace it with a vanity.

## CHOOSING A VANITY

If you have the space, get a large vanity. Not only will you have more storage, but you will gain more counter space by the sink.

For ease of installation and low maintenance, buy a unit with an integral sink and countertop, meaning that only one molded piece sits on top of the cabinet.

The cabinet should feel solid. Avoid units with doors made of particleboard. The cabinet should have a solid paint or polyurethane finish to protect against the humidity of a bathroom. A unit without a back will be easier to install than one with a plywood sheet that you have to cut for the plumbing.

For the countertop, synthetic marble may be your best bet. It is sturdy and has a surface that will stay shiny for years. Plastic and fiberglass will dull over time. Vitreous china is the best surface but is very expensive.

## REMOVE THE OLD SINK

Shut off the water at the stop valves below the sink. If there are no stop valves, shut off the water to the house and drain a faucet on a lower level. Set a bucket under the P-trap, and disassemble it with channel-type pliers or a pipe wrench. If it looks worn, plan on replacing it. Disconnect the supply lines at the stop valves.

If you have a wall-hung unit that just rests on a wall bracket, simply lift it up and out. If it doesn't budge, it may be connected to the bracket with bolts, which probably have rusted. Use a hacksaw to cut them.

## PREPARE THE PLUMBING

If you don't have stop valves under the sink, now is the time to install them; they come in

*You can choose among a large variety of cabinet styles and sink materials to find a vanity that fits your bathroom decor.*

## WHAT YOU'LL NEED

**MATERIALS:** vanity cabinet with top; faucet; supply lines; Teflon tape; sink tailpiece; P trap; shims, if needed; long screws.

**TOOLS:** channel-type pliers; pipe wrench; adjustable wrench; basin wrench; drill; saber saw; screwdriver; level; hacksaw.

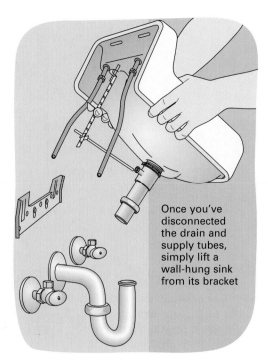

Once you've disconnected the drain and supply tubes, simply lift a wall-hung sink from its bracket

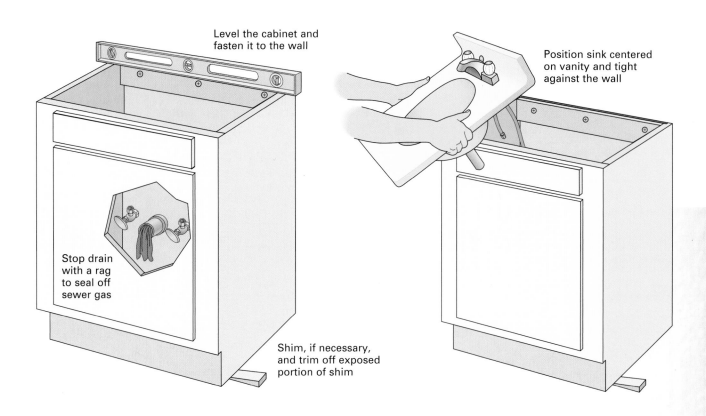

Level the cabinet and fasten it to the wall

Position sink centered on vanity and tight against the wall

Stop drain with a rag to seal off sewer gas

Shim, if necessary, and trim off exposed portion of shim

handy in emergencies. Choose an angle or straight stop made to fit your type of pipe. Install the valves and test by turning on the water. Measure to make sure the supply lines and the drain line will fit inside the cabinet. In most cases, this will not be a problem.

## SECURE THE CABINET

If your cabinet has a back, cut holes for the drain and the supply lines. It is often difficult to fit the pipes through small holes. Because the back will not be visible, you may want to make a large cutout that will easily accommodate all the plumbing. If pipes come up through the floor, you will need to cut precise holes in the bottom of the cabinet. For a neater job, use large drill bits rather than a saber saw, if possible.

Set the cabinet in place and check the top for level in both directions. If necessary, use shims at the floor or at the wall to make adjustments. Firmly attach the cabinet to the wall with screws driven into studs.

## INSTALL THE FAUCET AND SET THE TOP

Set the sink on its side and attach the faucet. Install flexible supply lines that are long enough to reach the stop valves; make sure

they are tight but do not overtighten. Install the drain and tailpiece, using plumber's putty where the outlet flange rests on the bottom of the sink. Install the pop-up drain assembly (*see page 49*).

Lift the sink carefully onto the cabinet and position it so it is centered from side to side and tight against the wall.

## ATTACH THE PLUMBING AND TEST

Crawl under the sink with a pair of channel-type pliers. Attach the supply lines to the stop valves and screw them on tight (*see page 49 for various types of supply lines*).

Install a new P-trap or reinstall the old one. Whether plastic or chrome, these pieces fit together with large nuts and rubber gaskets. Don't attempt to do without a P-trap—it's necessary to keep odors out of your bathroom. Attach the P-trap to the tailpiece and run the drain line out to the main drain line, which is usually positioned in the wall. Tighten all the nuts but avoid cranking down too hard.

Turn on the stops and look for leaks. Then turn on the faucet and watch the drain line for leaks. Finally, perform the ultimate test: Lift up the rod to stop up the sink and fill the bowl with water. Open the drain, and look carefully for drips. Tighten any leaking joints and retest until everything stays dry.

*Level and install the cabinet. Then install the faucet, supply lines, and drain before mounting the sink on the cabinet.*

*Special paint techniques truly express individuality in a personal room. In this bedroom, the soft edges of the diamond outlines on the walls beautifully contrast with the crisp fabrics.*

# PERSONAL ROOMS

A bedroom can be the most enjoyable room to improve because it is a personal space. That gives you the freedom to decorate it to reflect its occupant's personality without worrying about how it coordinates with the rest of the house. However, a bedroom can be challenging because it is usually a small space further restricted by doors, windows, and furniture. Bedrooms often have few architectural features or the space to accommodate them. No problem. Here are 10 clever ways to make a bedroom more attractive, comfortable, and efficient without spending a fortune. They range from decorating with special paint treatments to organizing closets. Each idea disguises an unsatisfactory or worn feature, highlights a good element, or adds character to a room.

# BORDER ON PERFECTION

With its continuous pattern, a border helps unify a room that is broken into small fragments by furniture and doors. Borders are easy to hang, so use them wherever you wish—at the ceiling line (called the frieze), at the soffit line or chair rail (called a dado when there is no molding), along baseboards, and around windows, doors, and large furniture.

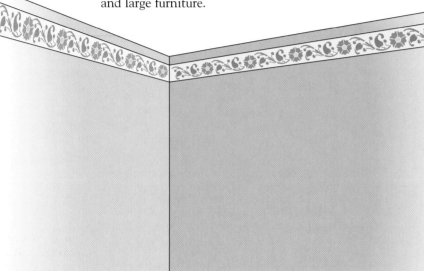

## PLAN THE LAYOUT

Most borders come in 5-yard rolls and have end-to-end patterns that join with a butt seam. (Nonmatching ends join with a double-cut seam.) Plan accordingly, allowing for ½ inch of material to be lost when you cut each inside corner and each double-cut seam. Start the layout in the least conspicuous corner of a room, where the pattern will not be matched at the seam.

## PLACE HORIZONTAL BORDERS

Continuous horizontal borders always run parallel to the ceiling line of a room. To ensure correct placement, use these guidelines.

■ **FRIEZE BORDERS:** Measure the width of the border. Mark this same distance from the ceiling at the ends of each wall. Snap a chalk line between the marks. The bottom edge of the border should align with the chalk line.

■ **DADO BORDERS:** The bottom edge of a dado is usually 32–33 inches above the floor, but a wide border is typically centered on a line 33 inches above the floor. Borders also can align with windowsills or large pieces of furniture. Decide on the height and subtract this distance from the height of the room. The result is your border's distance from the

*A continuous border helps give a unified feel to a room while adding a splash of color and design.*

## WHAT YOU'LL NEED

**MATERIALS:** border wallcoverings; paste; primer/sealer or sizing recommended for your material.

**TOOLS:** tape measure; pencil; chalk line; sharp utility knife; paste brush; water tray; stepladder; smoothing brush; framing square; straightedge; seam roller; sponges; towels.

*To install a border at the same time as wallpaper, paste and apply the border while the wallpaper is still wet. Cut along the bottom of the border with a straightedge and knife, lift up the border slightly, and remove the cutout piece of wallpaper.*

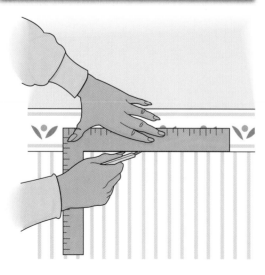

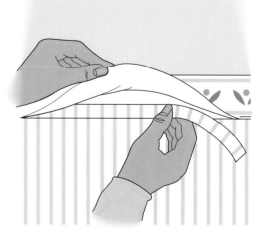

ceiling. Make light pencil marks on the ends of the walls at this distance from the ceiling, then snap a chalk line between the marks. The bottom edge of the border should align with this chalk line.

■ **BASEBOARD BORDERS:** Align the bottom edge of the border with the top of the baseboard.

## PLACE DOOR AND WINDOW BORDERS

Borders around openings follow the trim moldings. For a professional look, they require mitered right-angle corners. To do this, cut the lengths so they extend several inches beyond each other. Lay them on a worktable exactly as they will meet on the wall, with the horizontal lengths overlapping the vertical. Using a framing square, make sure they meet at a true 90-degree angle. Pressing firmly with a sharp knife to make sure you cut through both pieces at once, make a diagonal double-cut seam from the outside to the inside corners.

## HANG THE BORDERS

Prepare the border area by applying a wallcovering primer/sealer or sizing, following the package directions. (Ask a dealer for the best product, if you are not sure.) Cut the border sections to length.

Mix the paste, or purchase ready-mixed paste; in either case, use a product recommended for your material. Lay the border upside down on a flat surface, and apply paste with a paste brush, starting in the middle and working outward. Fold it accordion style, taking care not to wrinkle it. Let it set 3 to 5 minutes. For a prepasted border, soak it, fold it accordion style, and let it set for a few minutes, open. Then coat it with vinyl-to-vinyl paste.

Ideally, two people work together to hang a border. Unfolding the border 2 feet at a time, one feeds it to the other, who sets it in place with a smoothing brush.

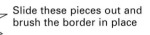

To make a miter-cut corner, check for square and slice with a sharp utility knife from corner to corner

Slide these pieces out and brush the border in place

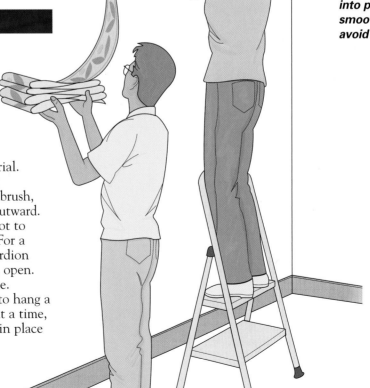

*Apply paste and fold the border accordion style. Carefully lift it into place and smooth it to avoid wrinkles.*

# PAINT WITH SPONGES

This versatile finish is quick and easy to apply. Colors are dabbed on the wall, creating a soft, dappled effect. Sponge light colors over a dark base, dark colors over a light base, or any other combination desired. Tone-on-tone pastels and neutrals work best for beginners. Use three top-coat colors in addition to the base color. Choose colors from the same family that are one to three tones apart on a color chip. Once the walls are prepared, allow one to two days to sponge a bedroom.

## PREPARE THE WALL

Repair any cracks and holes in the wall, filling with spackle and sanding and/or using spray-on crack sealer. Wash the walls with a heavy-duty cleaner, such as trisodium phosphate, or give them a light sanding. If you have stains, apply a coat of stain-killing primer/sealer.

Apply the base coat with a roller and brush for consistently complete coverage. Apply two coats if necessary.

Set up your work site so you can easily reach all parts of the walls without continually stopping to move something. For instance, use a small ladder that you can quickly move with one hand, rather than a large one that requires you to move everything in order to shift its position.

## LOAD THE SPONGE

For the sponge coats, you can use full-strength paint, a wash (1 part latex paint thinned with 5–9 parts water, depending on the translucency desired), or a glaze (alkyd paint thinned with equal parts of an oil glaze or glazing liquid and paint thinner).

Soak the sponge in water and wring it out until it is damp. Dip it in paint and dab off the excess on scrap paper.

To get the same amount of paint on the sponge each time, use a quart can. Loosen the lid and place it firmly back on top without pounding it tight. Tip the can upside down, then set it right side up again. Reopen the can and dab the sponge in the fresh paint on the inside of the lid.

*Sponging adds texture and depth to a wall, making it a one-of-a-kind creation.*

## WHAT YOU'LL NEED

**MATERIALS:** flat, eggshell, or satin finish latex or alkyd interior paint; spackle; spray-on crack sealer; heavy-duty cleaner; stain-killing primer/sealer; oil glaze or glazing liquid; paint thinner; mineral spirits; polyurethane finish.

**TOOLS:** plastic sheets and drop cloths; stepladder; roller with 3/16-inch or 1/4-inch nap sleeve; natural sea sponges with medium-size holes; sanding block; 120-grit sandpaper; paint trays; buckets; stirring sticks; paintbrush; scrap paper.

## APPLY TO THE WALL

Dab the sponge straight up and down on the wall. Do not twist or roll it. Make quick movements in a random pattern over the wall. Occasionally give the sponge a quarter turn clockwise to avoid producing an identifiable pattern. Work in areas about 4 feet square, randomly dabbing the sponge in spots about 12 inches apart so that the lighter-colored dabs will be mixed equally with the heavier dabs made soon after you have loaded the sponge. Allow plenty of base coat to show through this first sponge coat. Allow it to dry.

Apply the second color the same way, overlapping some of the first strokes. Let dry. Apply the third color, overlapping some of the first and second strokes and still letting some of the base color show through. Let dry.

If you find that you sponged too heavily in a spot, you can lighten the dark spot by sponging some of the base coat over it.

## FILLING IN CORNERS

If you try to dab all the way into a corner with a full-sized sponge, you may get an uneven appearance. Try using a 1-inch brush, dipping, wiping it off, and dabbing it as you did with the sponge. Or make a special corner sponge by cutting one edge of a piece of sponge that has the same-sized holes as the large sponge. Dip the uncut portion of the sponge and use it with the cut edge against the corner.

## APPLY FINAL WASH

Dilute the base color to a very thin wash (8 or 9 parts water to 1 part latex paint) or glaze (5 parts oil glaze or glazing liquid to 1 part each alkyd paint and paint thinner), and dab it over the topcoats to blend the colors. Or apply a coat of satin finish polyurethane that has been thinned with mineral spirits.

*Dip the sponge, gently wipe off the excess, and apply to the wall in evenly spaced dabs.*

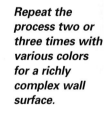

*Repeat the process two or three times with various colors for a richly complex wall surface.*

# RAG-ROLL A WALL

Rag-rolling is one of the bolder ways to finish a wall. It is similar in technique to sponging, but you use rolled-up rags to give walls a sophisticated texture. Because of its somewhat complex effect, rag-rolling does a wonderful job of hiding imperfections in a wall.

There are fewer color rules with this technique than with other faux painting methods. Roll light colors over a dark base coat or vice versa. Don't hesitate to mix colors that are very different from each other; experiment on a piece of paper to find exciting combinations. After preparing the walls, count on spending one or two days applying the base coat and two or three rag-roll coats.

## PREPARE THE WALLS AND APPLY A BASE COAT

Spread drop cloths or plastic sheets on the floors because this will be a messy project.

Although the technique will camouflage small imperfections in the walls, you still need to fill in cracks and holes with spackle or spray-on crack sealer. Wash the walls with a heavy-duty cleaner or give them a light sanding throughout. If there are stains, apply a coat of stain-killing sealer/primer.

Apply a coat of base paint. Use a roller and a brush and completely cover the walls; apply two coats if necessary.

## LOAD THE RAG AND ROLL

Use rags of the same material throughout the project. Dip the rag in paint and wring it out slightly. Then twist or bunch it into a roll. Before you start on the wall, experiment on scrap pieces of plywood or large sheets of paper.

Slowly roll the paint-dipped rag. Start in a corner. Work from the bottom to the top. Let plenty of the base color show. Use two hands, and vary the direction and pressure from time to time to avoid uniformity.

Roll the next area beside the first and continue until the wall is complete. Let the paint dry and repeat with a new color. Make each additional rag-roll coat overlap the previous strokes. Let the paint dry.

## APPLY FINAL WASH

Dilute the base color to a very thin wash (8 or 9 parts water to 1 part latex paint) or glaze (5 parts oil glaze or glazing liquid to 1 part each alkyd paint and paint thinner). Apply it with a roller and brush over the entire wall. This will help blend the colors together.

*A rag-rolled wall is fancier than sponging and a great way to express your taste.*

## WHAT YOU'LL NEED

**MATERIALS:** flat, eggshell, or satin finish latex or alkyd interior paint; spray-on crack sealer; spackle; trisodium phosphate or other strong cleaner; stain-killing primer/sealer; polyurethane finish; oil glaze; glazing liquid; thinner.

**TOOLS:** plastic sheets; drop cloths; stepladder; roller with 3/16-inch or 1/4-inch-nap; 1½- or 2-foot squares of lint-free rags; paint trays; putty knife; buckets; sanding block; 120-grit sandpaper; stirring sticks; scrap paper or plywood; finish brush.

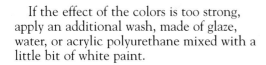

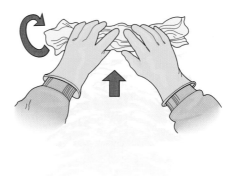

If the effect of the colors is too strong, apply an additional wash, made of glaze, water, or acrylic polyurethane mixed with a little bit of white paint.

## VARIATION: CORDUROY RAGGING

This technique produces a series of short, thin lines going in all directions. It makes a wall seem textured, like a piece of rough cloth.

Cut pieces of wide-wale corduroy into 12-inch squares. Cut with pinking shears, to minimize fraying. (If small pieces of lint get into the paint, it will be hard to get the look you want.) Wash and dry the pieces, and use masking tape to remove all the lint.

Although you can use the technique with latex paint, it works best with a mixture of 3 parts glazing liquid to 1 part oil-based paint. This can be applied over a base coat of latex paint. Pour only a small amount of the glaze or paint into a tray for dipping so that if it gets infested with lint you will need to discard only a little.

Bunch up the section of corduroy as if it were a small pillow, with the cut ends tucked away. Dip it lightly into paint and test on a piece of paper. Press the cloth lightly against the wall in a series of dabbing motions so that the pattern of the fabric is visible. Lift and twist between strokes to produce a series of lines going in all different directions. Dab all over the wall in widely spaced applications so that darker and lighter imprints will be spread out randomly.

If a rag becomes thoroughly soaked with glaze or paint, it will be difficult to get the imprint of the cloth on the wall. You may be able to correct this by wringing out the rag thoroughly, but it is best to discard it and start with a new rag.

*Dip the rag, wring out, and roll on the wall.*

*Apply in vertical columns from floor to ceiling, then fill in with successive coats.*

# DECORATE BY SPATTERING AND DRAGGING

There are several ways to decorate wall surfaces without worrying about precise techniques. You also can come up with some creative ideas of your own. As with the other techniques, choosing the right colors is key. Select closely related colors for a subtle effect or experiment to find a combination of different hues that you like to see together.

**Simple paint techniques can be easier than applying wall covering and every bit as decorative.**

To spatter a wall, use a rough-textured tool dipped lightly in paint to apply little dots and splotches of various colors. Dragging means that you apply glaze to a wall and then remove part of it with a textured or corrugated tool. For either technique, plan on spending a day applying the finish to a wall that has been prepared and given a base coat.

## SPATTERING

The instructions here show two ways to spatter—one wild and messy (and great for kids) and the other controlled and tidy. Both are fun in their own ways. The first is spontaneous, allowing you or your child to go crazy throwing paint around. The second is nearly meditative and soothing.

## FREE SPATTERING

A free and loose spattering approach can be fun for you, or it can be a great way to have a child help paint his or her own room. (It will mean hours of work for you and about 15 minutes of fun for your child, but they will be memorable minutes.)

After the base coat is applied and dry, cover absolutely everything that you do not want spattered. Mask the woodwork unless you want it spattered too. Use pieces of cardboard for the windows and doors. Make sure the floor is completely covered.

Open a small can of paint. Dip a brush in the can, then spray the paint around the room willy-nilly, using helicopterlike motions.

There is no need to wait for the first spatter coat to dry before moving on to the next. Spatter on two or three coats. Let the paint dry and remove all the masking tape.

## CONTROLLED SPATTERING

This technique goes fairly quickly and is one of the most clever faux techniques. The base coat will predominate, with the spatterings acting as accents. First, choose a tool: You can use a large paintbrush or a pad made for cleaning grills. Anything with a rough texture will do; experiment on pieces of paper before working on a wall.

## WHAT YOU'LL NEED

**MATERIALS:** flat, eggshell, or satin finish latex interior paint; spray-on crack sealer; spackle; trisodium phosphate or other heavy-duty cleaner; stain-killing primer/sealer; oil glaze or glazing liquid if needed; polyurethane finish.

**TOOLS:** plastic sheets; drop cloths; stepladder; masking tape; scrap paper or plywood; roller with 3/16-inch or 1/4-inch nap; paint trays; buckets; putty knife; sanding block; 120-grit sandpaper; stirring sticks; paintbrush; large brush, paint-stripping or grill-cleaning pad, or other rough-textured tool for spattering; graining comb, stiff brush, pieces of corrugated cardboard, or notched trowel for dragging.

For either technique, start with a smooth, stain-free wall painted with a base coat (*see page 58*).

After the base coat is dry, mix a glaze of 3 parts glaze to 1 part paint. Pour a little into a paint tray, and dip your tool lightly into the paint. Touch it to a dry area of the pan to get rid of excess. Dab it onto the wall over a large area. Repeat and stand back every once in a while to see that you are getting fairly consistent coverage. Repeat for the other colors.

## DRAGGING

With this technique, you apply paint and then remove some of it to make a pattern. It involves only one glaze color over a base coat, so the visual interest comes from the pattern rather than from multiple colors. Dragging is a good way to hide the grooves in painted paneling.

## MAKE A TOOL AND TEST

The tool you use will determine the look of the wall. Mix a glaze and experiment with different tools and strokes on a piece of plywood or a large piece of paper.

One of the more effective tools is made by cutting corrugated cardboard into 1-foot-wide pieces and then pulling off the paper on one side. The corrugations will then be exposed and can be used to make a series of lines. Make a number of these tools; once one gets soaked, it becomes ineffective.

Other options include a squeegee that has been notched (*see page 19*) or a notched trowel designed for spreading floor-tile adhesive (*see page 7*). A stiff-bristled brush or broom also can be used to produce finer lines that are random.

## ROLL AND DRAG

Mix the glaze and apply it with a roller. You will have to use a brush in corners and close to moldings. Work quickly and cover an area about 4 feet wide from ceiling to floor. How thickly you should apply the glaze depends on your tool; if it is too thick, you will end up with big globs at the end of a stroke.

Hold the tool with two hands. Start at the top of the wall and pull the tool down. Or make a checkerboard pattern by dragging down and then across.

Grill-cleaning tool

*For a spattered effect, dip a grill-cleaning tool into a puddle of glaze, blot it, and dab the wall.*

*For dragging, use a piece of corrugated cardboard with one outer surface torn off.*

# CREATE A STENCILED CANVAS FLOORCLOTH

The forerunner of linoleum, hand-painted canvas floorcloths offer an inexpensive and practical way to create a floor covering that is as durable and easy to clean as it is decorative. They look particularly lovely on hardwood and ceramic tile floors in country-style and informal homes. They also let you be the artist, designing exactly the pattern you want in your favorite colors.

## CHOOSE OR CREATE A DESIGN

A floorcloth can be as small as a 2×3-foot area rug or as large as an 8×10-foot carpet (or even larger). Draw the measurements to scale on graph paper and sketch out possible designs. Study interior decorating, design, folk art, and stencil pattern books for inspiration. Make your pattern as traditional or as fanciful as you please. Bold and simple patterns are more effective. Geometric patterns look especially good.

Or go to a crafts store and look for stencils. You may end up combining several stencils to make your own design in a consistently repeating pattern. Or you may use one type of stencil in the corner, another around the edge, and another near the middle. The possibilities are nearly endless.

To make your own stencil, buy sheets of acetate from a crafts store. Draw designs on the acetate with a pencil, then cut them out with a sharp utility knife.

If you will be repeating the same stenciled design in different colors, get or make a separate stencil for each color.

*An old-fashioned floorcloth will show off your creativity, whether you use store-bought stencils, make your own, or paint directly on the fabric.*

## WHAT YOU'LL NEED

**MATERIALS:** preprimed artist's canvas; fabric-to-fabric glue; tinted primer, if needed; flat latex interior paint; clear acrylic varnish or polyurethane; heavy mercerized cotton thread, if needed.

**TOOLS:** plastic sheets; drop cloths; tape measure; pencil; graph paper; acetate; utility knife; sewing machine and No. 18 machine needle, if needed; masking tape; synthetic bristle paintbrushes; artist's brushes; stenciling brush; paint trays; chalkline or straightedge; scrap paper.

## PREPARE THE CANVAS

Add 3 inches for hems to each dimension to figure the gross size. Order preprimed artist's canvas in that size from an art supply store. If you want an exceptionally heavy, durable floorcloth, use a double layer of canvas.

Lay the canvas, right side down, on a flat surface protected from paint splatters. Turn under 1½-inch-wide hems on each side, mitering the corners. Seal with fabric-to-fabric glue. If you prefer, sew the hems on a home sewing machine with a No. 18 needle and heavy-duty mercerized cotton thread at eight stitches per inch. Take a large double-layer floorcloth to an automobile upholstery shop for hemming.

## COAT WITH PRIMER

If you like the natural color of canvas, simply paint the stencil design directly on it. In that case, be sure to give the floorcloth a heavy coating of polyurethane at the end because the light color will not hide dirt satisfactorily.

Lay the canvas on a flat surface that has been covered with a dropcloth or protective sheets of plastic.

If the background color is dark, ask a paint supplier to tint some latex primer so it approximates the color. Apply the primer and allow to dry before applying the base coat.

With a large brush, paint on a base coat of flat latex paint. Work to get a consistent texture. Ideally, the canvas will be completely covered with paint, yet the texture of the fabric will show through. Allow the paint to dry for at least 24 hours.

## STENCIL OR DRAW A DESIGN

To hand-paint a design, use high-quality artist's brushes. Draw the design with faint pencil marks or at least draw lines that indicate the general outlines of the design. Apply the paint using long, fluid strokes wherever possible.

To apply a stencil, first mark out the general layout with faint pencil lines; a straightedge or chalkline may help. Affix the stencil to the cloth with masking tape.

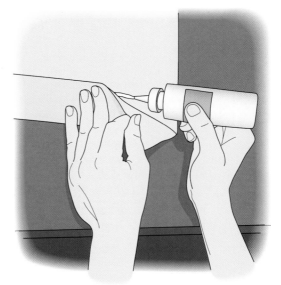

*Hem the canvas by folding over the edge and adhering it with fabric-to-fabric glue.*

Using a standard stenciling brush may cause problems if the base coat is still soft (latex paint often stays soft for a week or two after drying). A standard 1-inch brush may work better.

Dip the brush into the paint and remove the excess on scraps of paper. Apply it with pouncing strokes, straight up and down. Either fill the open area completely with paint or fill the outer edges completely, then go over the inside portion lightly.

Let the paint dry for three days. Then seal well by brushing on seven coats of acrylic varnish or polyurethane finish, letting each coat dry before applying the next. Let the final coat dry five days before walking on the floorcloth.

*Working around the cloth, dab the paint into the stencil.*

# ADD A CEILING FAN

Bedroom ceiling fans make sleeping comfortable on all but the hottest nights. They also cost much less to operate than air conditioning.

Before you begin, check local electrical code requirements. If you have any doubt about your ability to wire the fan, hire a licensed electrician to do the job.

"Ceiling-hugging" fans may seem like a good idea for rooms with 8-foot ceilings, and they are often the cheapest alternatives. But if the fan blades measure less than 10 inches from the ceiling, the fan will barely create a breeze even at high speed. Purchase a model with a down pipe. Be sure the fan has a light kit, too.

*A ceiling fan is pleasant to look at as well as being a good way to save on air-conditioning bills.*

### CHOOSE A FAN AND LOCATE IT

A dealer can help you select a fan properly sized for your room. Decide whether you want one with a light fixture, as well. Ideally, the fan will be centered in the room.

Wherever you install the fan, the lowest edge of its blades must be at least 7 feet above the floor, and the blade tips must be at least 24 inches away from any wall. Do not hang a fan below, next to, or between air ducts, beams, or other obstructions that can interfere with its air flow.

If you're not replacing a light, then locate a point between ceiling joists close to the center of the ceiling. Find this point and make a cutout in the ceiling slightly larger than the size of the electrical box.

### PREPARE THE ELECTRICAL BOX

If the new fan/light will replace a ceiling light fixture, remove the fixture and examine the electrical box. It must be firmly attached and not wiggle easily when you grab it. The type of box matters less than whether it will be able to withstand years of vibrating and to bear the weight of the fan. Making the box secure may be the most difficult part of your job.

If you have access from an unfinished attic space above, work from there to minimize damage to your ceiling. Reinforce the existing box by cutting a 2×4 to fit snugly between joists and attaching it with screws tight against the top of the box. Then drive screws through the box and into the 2×4. Or buy a new electrical box equipped with a brace and attach the brace to the joists. If you have any doubts, buy a UL-approved box designed for use with a ceiling fan.

## WHAT YOU'LL NEED

**MATERIALS:** fan with light kit, fan brace or 2×4, if electrical box is not strong; electrician's tape; twist-on wire connectors; ceiling fan box, if needed; screws and a strap for attaching fan; approved cable, switch, switchplate, if needed.

**TOOLS:** drill; tape measure; wallboard or keyhole saw; hammer; screwdriver; wire stripper; level; ladder.

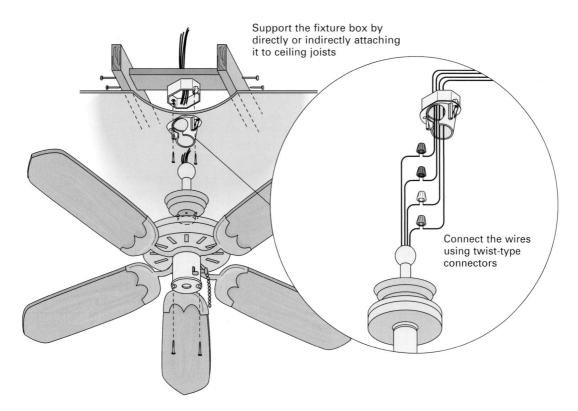

Support the fixture box by directly or indirectly attaching it to ceiling joists

Connect the wires using twist-type connectors

If you have no access from above and need to strengthen the box, purchase a special brace designed for the purpose. You will have to cut a hole in the ceiling to install it. Patch and paint the ceiling before installing the fan.

If the ceiling box already is controlled by a wall switch, you will have no major electrical work to do. If you have a ceiling fixture controlled by a pull chain, you can leave it or run electrical cable to the wall and install a switch. If you need a new box, consult with or hire an electrician.

## ATTACH THE BRACKET

Turn off the power. Install the socket hanger or hanger bracket for the fan according to the manufacturer's instructions. Some fans call for the hanger to be screwed to the double ears of the box with the mounting screws, locknuts, and washers provided. Other fans are attached to the framing, not the box.

Most fans have a hook arrangement that allows you to hang the fan motor temporarily in place while you wire it.

## WIRE THE FAN

If you have old wiring in the ceiling box, inspect it carefully for damage. Cover any cracked or frayed insulation completely with electrician's tape. If the wiring going into the box is damaged, consult with an electrician to remedy this dangerous situation. Strip the tips of the wires.

For new wiring, make sure that the cable is secured with a cable clamp and that 8 inches or so stick out. Strip the cable sheathing to within 1 inch or so of the box. Strip the tips of the wires.

Connecting the wires is usually simple. If you have a light kit, you will probably twist the fan's blue wire with its black wire and attach that to the house's black wire. Hook white to white and ground to ground. Use twist-type connectors for all the connections.

Because fans vibrate, parts of the wiring inside a fan box sometimes make noise by vibrating against the box or each other. Use electrical tape to tie the wiring tightly and out of the way.

## INSTALL CANOPY AND BLADES

Screw the fan body and the canopy in place according to the manufacturer's directions. Attaching the fan blades will take some time. Attach the blade irons to the fan blades then to the motor. Install the light kit, too, if it is not already attached to the fan motor.

If the fan wobbles, first check that all the screws are tight. Then make sure it is hanging straight down; use a small level to check the down rod for plumb. Then take the blades down and see whether one is warped. If so, take back the entire set and have them replaced. If one of the blade irons is twisted, do the same. If the fan motor wobbles when it is running without blades attached, it is defective and should be replaced.

# FIND HIDDEN SPACE IN A SMALL CLOSET

An inefficient bedroom closet is frustrating. It slows you down in the mornings by making you hunt for needed items. Also, clothes tend to get squished and wrinkled because they are crammed together.

*This 6-foot-wide closet has hanging areas designed for clothing of three different lengths, as well as a shoe rack and shelves. By mapping needs and planning accordingly, you waste little space, and your clothes will not be rumpled.*

Transform a closet quickly, easily, and inexpensively by installing a modular closet system. Such a system works its organizing magic just as well in hall or linen closets.

The instructions here show how to organize a 6-foot-wide closet using wire shelves and rods. (*Pages 68–69 show how to organize a larger closet using solid-wood products.*) You will need a day or two to plan, purchase, and install wire rods and shelves for a small bedroom closet.

## WHAT YOU'LL NEED

**MATERIALS:** wire shelves with hanging rods; vertical support poles; hanging brackets with screws.

**TOOLS:** tape measure; graph paper; pencil; level; stud finder; drill; hacksaw; screwdriver bit; screwdriver; hammer.

## MAP YOUR NEEDS

The standard closet arrangement, with a single hanging rod and a shelf or two above it, is extremely wasteful of space. If you plan a system carefully, you can double the amount of storage area available. The key is to tailor the space so that it will hold specific items of clothing, accessories, and other storage items.

Start by itemizing the number, size, and shape of everything stored in the closet. List, for example, shirts, jackets, slacks, and coats. Line up the shoes and decide how much shoe-rack space you need. Stack linens and sweaters, and measure the piles. Place long-term storage items in boxes and note the dimensions of the boxes. Not only list what you have, but also try to estimate any new storage needs you may require in the next few years. One advantage in making such a list is that you may discover rarely used items that really belong in the basement, garage, or a charity box.

Measure the closet: front to back, side to side, floor to ceiling, and door widths and heights. Draw the closet width and height measurements on graph paper.

Use the recommended storage heights (*see page 68*) to sketch out the closet arrangement. Plan to use two hanging sections for short clothing, such as shirts and slacks. Hang long garments in full-length sections. Install high shelves for seldom-used items, such as seasonal clothing and blankets. If space permits, separate major sections with vertical sections of stacked shelves or drawers. Place shoe racks close to the floor.

## PRODUCTS TO BUY

There are many competing storage systems and products, so take a look at several systems before deciding. In most cases, you can buy complete systems that include shelves, rods, and the hardware needed to install them. They also come with a host of storage accessories, such as tie racks and shoe racks.

There are two main types of do-it-yourself systems: those made of ventilating coated-wire components and those made of solid particleboard components with a high-pressure-plastic laminate. These instructions apply to coated-wire components.

Instead of buying the hanging rod separately from the shelves, it usually makes more sense to buy a shelf that incorporates a hanging rod. Avoid rods that will not allow you to slide the hangers from side to side.

It's a good idea to have a few hooks but not too many or your closet will look messy. They usually work best on the back of a door; use a few for robes, pajamas, and other frequently used items.

Wire slide-out drawers can be handy for large items, such as sweaters, but for smaller items or things you don't want to look at, such as socks and underwear, use a dresser or purchase a solid-wood drawer unit (*see pages 68–69*). Slide-out drawers may not be worth the cost; simple and cheap shelving usually work just as well.

## INSTALL WIRE SHELVES AND RODS

Recheck the closet measurements for precise accuracy if you want a dealer to cut the shelves for you. Go to a home center with your plan and decide on the products appropriate to your closet.

Be sure the dealer sells you everything required. You also need to have vertical poles that support the horizontal shelf/rods wherever you change the shelving or at least every 3 to 4 feet to prevent sagging. There are clips for attaching shelves to closet walls, clips for attaching shelves to poles, and end brackets for attaching the forward end of a shelf to a side wall. You will need screws for the clips and anchors for attaching the screws in case you do not hit a stud.

Ask the dealer to cut some or all of the pieces. Or cut them yourself with a hacksaw. Manufacturer's directions will tell you how to take into account the thicknesses of end brackets when measuring for cutting.

Use a level and a pencil to make faint lines in the back of the closet showing where the shelves will go. Use a stud finder to locate the studs. Cut a shelf, slip on the end bracket, and have a helper hold it in place while you check for level and attach. Set the level on top of the shelf and position a clip so that the screw will drive into a stud. Drive the screw, using a drill equipped with a screwdriver bit. If you need to install clips where there is no stud, use plastic wallboard anchors.

Attach the uprights as you go, checking that they are level from front to back as well as from side to side.

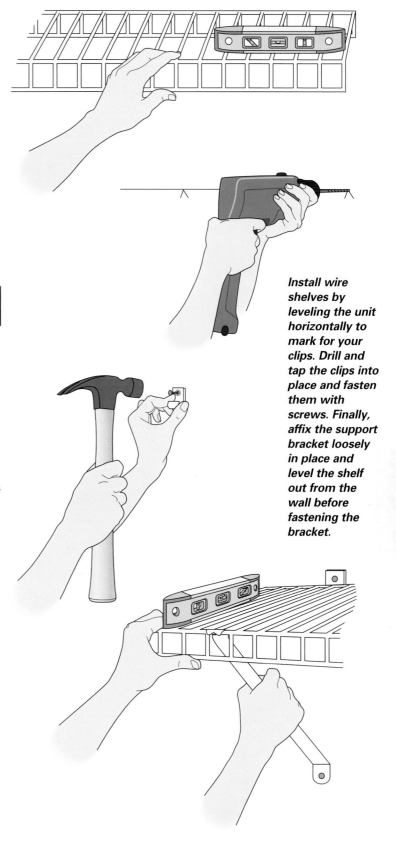

**Install wire shelves by leveling the unit horizontally to mark for your clips. Drill and tap the clips into place and fasten them with screws. Finally, affix the support bracket loosely in place and level the shelf out from the wall before fastening the bracket.**

# MAXIMIZE A LARGE CLOSET

The bigger the closet, the more possibilities for areas designed just for your needs. A large his-and-her closet can be set up to forestall arguments and restore marital bliss. Or it can be used to house an expansive wardrobe.

You can build your own components, using plywood or boards for the shelves and wood hanging rods. It will save you some money but

*A large closet like this one can eliminate the need for a dresser, freeing up space in the bedroom.*

## WHAT YOU'LL NEED

**MATERIALS:** wire shelves with closet rods; laminated wooden drawer and shelf units; vertical support poles; hanging brackets with screws; shims if needed.

**TOOLS:** tape measure; graph paper; pencil; level; stud finder; drill; hammer; screwdriver bit; screwdriver; hacksaw.

may not be worth the time spent cutting and painting. (Painting can take longer than building, especially if you have a number of short shelves.) Building your own drawers requires extra time and tools.

Mixing solid-wood components with wire shelves and rods makes sense for a lot of people because there are some items they want to look at and others they would like to store. Planning and installing a closet like this will take about two days.

## PLANNING A LARGE CLOSET

Many of the principles that apply to small closets apply here (*see page 66*). Plan by itemizing your clothing and other belongings to be stored then map out the new closet using graph paper.

It often helps to divide a large closet in half or in thirds to make it easier to find things. If two people share the closet, then naturally you can divide it by person. Or you may want to reserve part of the closet for casual clothes and the other part for formal attire or work clothes. Or use half for clothes and the other half to meet storage needs.

In most cases the easiest way to plan is to start with a shelf or drawer unit somewhere in the middle. Add shelving areas of various sizes on either side until you have made room for all your hanging clothes. Then find room for shoes, ties, boxes, and other items.

If you have a functional but plain dresser, save money and effort by simply placing it in

## COMMON CLOTHING SIZES

When mapping out your closet space, keep in mind these standard clothing sizes. In order to stay unwrinkled, clothes need elbow room, as well as enough vertical space to hang freely.

| Item | Width | Length |
|---|---|---|
| Man's or woman's suit | 2½" | 42" |
| Dress | 2" | 60" |
| Slacks folded over hanger | 1½" | 34" |
| Man's shirt | 1¼" | 38" |
| Woman's blouse | 1¼" | 34" |
| Skirt | 1½" | 36" |

the closet and perhaps painting it white to match the components. Measure for the other components as if the dresser were a permanent part of the space.

## OTHER STORAGE OPTIONS

A variety of laminated wood storage components are available. Among them:

■ **DRAWERS:** A stack of drawers makes it easy to store and access small items. Combine small drawers for socks with large drawers for bulkier items. A shelf unit with drawers keeps sweaters and linens dust free.

■ **HAMPER:** A pull-out hamper is convenient for laundry. Dirty clothes can be tossed into the hamper, which can be carried to the washing machine. Two hampers can be used to keep colors separated from whites.

■ **STORAGE CONTAINERS:** Equipped with tight-fitting lids, stackable plastic bins keep items dust free for long-term storage.

■ **SHOE RACKS:** Revolving shoe racks are ideal for people with lots of shoes. Typically, an 8-foot-tall pole that is 16 inches wide will hold up to 24 pairs of shoes.

■ **BELT RACKS:** Slide-out belt racks and tie racks keep these hard-to-store small items in good shape.

■ **FILE CABINETS:** Roll-out file cabinets hold hanging files—the easiest kind to use— and can be easily transported from your work area to the closet.

## INSTALLING DRAWER UNITS AND SHELVES

Bring your drawing, with exact dimensions, to a home center or other supplier. If you are sure of your measurements, the dealer can cut the components on the spot. Otherwise, count on cutting the wire units with a hacksaw—normally you will not need to cut any of the wood components.

Set the wood components in place and check for level. Use shims if a component is not level in both directions to ensure that drawers and doors will operate easily.

Install the wire components (*follow the directions on page 67*). In some cases, you will attach end brackets to a wood unit. Be sure to drill the right-sized pilot hole before driving screws because particleboard cracks easily.

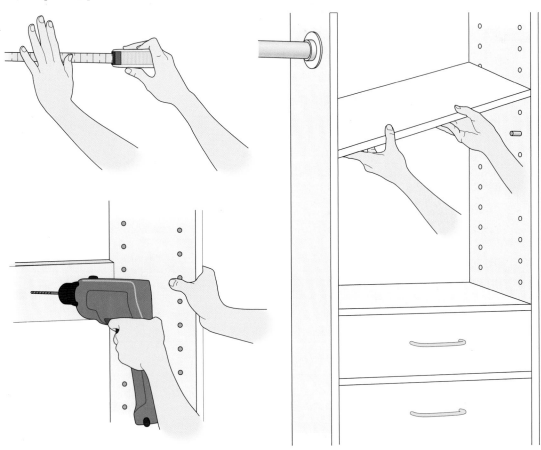

*Measure and mark the location of all your closet units before installing them. Level and fasten them in place, then add closet rods and shelves.*

# REFLECT ON A DOOR MIRROR

A full-length mirror on the inside of a bedroom closet, bathroom closet, or hall linen closet door provides a convenient, discreet accessory.

Begin by measuring the door. Buy a flat-edge mirror approximately 10 inches narrower and 15 inches shorter than the door. It should have finished edges if you are not installing trim. There are two installation options: Attach the mirror to the door with mastic or tape or attach with mirror clips. With the first option, you can add trim. The project will take a few hours.

## INSTALL WITH GLUE OR TAPE, AND ADD TRIM

Take the door off its hinges and lay it flat, back side up. If it is bare wood or a porous material, seal it with primer and paint, or coat with polyurethane. Otherwise, clean it with trisodium phosphate or another heavy-duty cleaner. Rinse the door with water containing ¼ cup white vinegar per gallon. Dry it with a towel, then let it dry for 24 hours.

Wipe the back of the mirror with isopropyl alcohol. Using mirror mastic or mirror mounting tape according to the manufacturer's directions, press the mirror in place on the door. Shim to stabilize it if the door is not perfectly flat.

To trim the mirror with molding, choose a molding that will fit over the mirror, such as picture-frame molding. Miter-cut the corners, and install by carefully driving 3-penny nails. Set the nails, fill, and paint or stain.

## OR INSTALL WITH MIRROR CLIPS

You can do this without taking the door down. Have a helper hold the mirror in place, parallel with the edge of the door. Using a drill with a screwdriver bit, hold in place a clip at the bottom of the door and drive the screw so it is just snug to the mirror—don't overtighten. Install at least one more clip at the bottom and six or seven more around the perimeter of the mirror. If the mirror rattles a bit, use a screwdriver to tighten the screws.

*An inexpensive full-length mirror, affixed to the inside of a closet door, stays out of sight until needed.*

## WHAT YOU'LL NEED

**MATERIALS:** mirror with or without wood frame; glass cleaner; TSP or other heavy-duty cleaner; white vinegar; isopropyl alcohol; primer and paint or polyurethane; mirror mastic or mounting tape, picture-frame molding, 3d finishing nails, and wood filler, for gluing mirror; or mirror clips with screws.

**TOOLS:** tape measure; hand or power drill; hammer; towels; rags.

# HANG ADJUSTABLE SHELVES

This is probably the simplest way to hang shelves on a wall. If you buy high-quality components, the shelves can be attractive, as well.

The shelves, though simple, must be hung correctly, or they may pull out of the wall when heavy objects are placed on them. If you are using 1×10s for the shelves, support them with standards and brackets every 24 inches, or they eventually will sag. Installing a set of shelves like the one shown will take several hours.

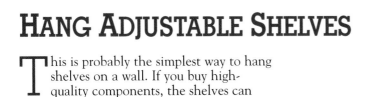

## INSTALL STANDARDS

Use a stud finder to locate the studs in the walls. Hammer in small finishing nails to make sure you've found them.

Hold the first standard at the desired height (make sure it is right side up), and drive a screw through the top hole and into the stud. Use the level to make sure the standard is plumb and drive screws in the other holes.

It is important to install the other standards at the same height as the first. Set a level on top of the first standard or use a straight board with a level on top of it if your level is not long enough. Use a pencil to mark where the tops of the other standards should be placed. Install them as you did the first.

## WHAT YOU'LL NEED

**MATERIALS:** standards; brackets; lumber; screws; paint or stain; polyurethane.

**TOOLS:** drill; screwdriver bit; stud finder; level; pencil.

## HOOK UP BRACKETS AND SHELVES

Slide the brackets into the standards at the desired heights—count bracket holes to ensure they are at the same height. The brackets should snap into place as you push down on them.

Cut all the shelves to the same length or vary the length for a decorative touch. They should not extend more than 8 inches past either outside bracket. Paint or apply stain and polyurethane finish. Because these shelves do not have side pieces, you may need to use bookends on both sides.

*A simple set of adjustable shelves is practical and can appear interesting, if it is well painted and the objects attractively arranged.*

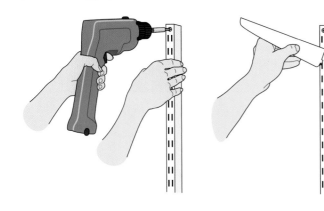

*Install the first standard, make sure it is plumb, and install the others to the same height. Clip in the brackets and set shelves on top, or attach with screws if the brackets provide mounting holes.*

*Even small projects like fences and arbors can add up to give a home a dramatic presence. The crisp, white curves of these outdoor structures not only are architectural enhancements but also create a setting for stunning plantings.*

# CURB APPEAL

Real estate agents know the importance of the first impression of a house: In just 15 seconds, potential buyers decide whether they like it or not. The decision is based on overall appearance; if it's negative, nothing is likely to change their minds. In the parlance of professionals, a house that gives a good first impression has "curb appeal." Part of that first impression is based on style, which you can't easily change. The rest is based on things you can improve: condition of the exterior, color scheme, landscaping, and individual features that give a home personality. This chapter focuses on those features. They're simple touches—a romantic arbor, a brick patio, a trellis that frames a front door. There are shutters to cheer up windows, flower boxes to bring living color to a yard, and easy-to-install lights that accent the beauty of home and lawn.

# ADD AN ENTRY TRELLIS

Framing an entry door with a latticework trellis is a quick, inexpensive way to add charm to a house. Flowering vines on a trellis give the house a country-cottage image. If you purchase a ready-made plastic or painted trellis, it will take only a couple of hours to install. Making and painting lattice panels using premade lattice sheets will take about half a day. If you start from scratch and build your own lattice panels, you will probably need a whole day.

## CHOOSE A LATTICE STYLE

The front door is a focal point, so take time to decide on the type of lattice that will look best. If the door is formal, smooth, well-painted wood that runs vertically and horizontally is often the best choice. Or plan to make a geometric pattern that mimics some aspect of the exterior. For an informal look, consider selecting rough-sawn wood and possibly running the lattice boards diagonally.

Choose the climbing plant at the same time you plan the design. A bushy plant with thick branches, such as a rose bush, needs wide-spaced lattice. More delicate plants that shoot out tendrils almost overnight, such as clematis, are easy to maintain if the lattice pieces are close together.

You have three options:
■ Purchase a lattice panel that is ready to be installed. It should be resistant to the weather—plastic or well-painted wood are two possibilities. Home centers have a variety of styles available.
■ Purchase a 2×8-foot or 4×8-foot sheet of lattice, cut it to size, and build a frame. The sheets are typically made of pressure-treated wood or redwood. Choose a sheet that is a full ¾ inch thick (that is, made of pieces ⅜ inch thick) because a thinner sheet will not be sturdy.
■ Make your own lattice, using 1×2s, or have a lumberyard rip-cut some pieces that are ¾×¾ inches. This will be only a little more work than the second option.

Decide on the finish, as well. White paint provides a classic look. The frame, if any, can be painted the color of the house siding and the trellis, the color of the house trim. If you are using redwood or another good-looking

*A simple trellis with vines dramatically improves the appearance of an entry door.*

## WHAT YOU'LL NEED

**MATERIALS:** factory-made lattice panel or lattice sheet with 1×2s for frame or rot-resistant lattice materials; decking screws or galvanized box nails; copper or plastic pipe or washers for spacers; plastic anchors, if needed; primer; exterior paint; mineral spirits, if needed.

**TOOLS:** tape measure; chalk line; pencil; circular saw; drill; hammer; paintbrush; framing square.

rot-resistant wood, consider staining it and then coating it with a water-repelling sealer. If you like the look of redwood that has turned gray with age, coat it only with clear water-repelling sealer. Once the trellis is covered with plants, it will be difficult to paint or treat, so do a thorough job.

## INSTALL READY-MADE LATTICE PANELS

If the panels are not already the correct length, cut them—they probably will look best if they are as high as the top of the trim molding over the door. The lattice need not extend all the way to the ground. Put the cut end at the bottom so the top of the panel looks finished.

Unless you are attaching a plastic lattice panel to vinyl or aluminum siding, do not attach the panel directly to the house. Water will collect and sit wherever the lattice is tight to the house, possibly causing both the lattice and the siding to rot. Instead, use spacers to hold the lattice away from the house by $\frac{1}{2}$ inch or so wherever a nail or screw is driven.

Make spacers by cutting pieces of copper or plastic pipe with a hacksaw. Or use four zinc washers for each spacer. Install by drilling pilot holes and driving screws through the lattice and the spacers and into the house. If you have a masonry wall, drill holes with a masonry bit, tap in plastic anchors, and drive in screws.

outside pieces for evenly spaced horizontal strips. Cut the horizontals, set them in place, and attach by drilling a pilot hole and driving a $1\frac{1}{4}$-inch decking screw at each joint. Attach to the house with spacers.

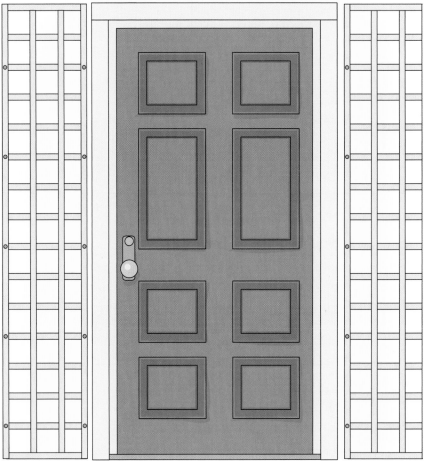

## USE LATTICE SHEETS

Set the sheet on several long pieces of lumber, mark with a chalk line, and cut with a circular saw. Cut pieces of 1×2 to form a frame that is 2–3 inches shorter than the lattice in both directions. Set the 1×2s on a flat surface, lay the lattice on top, and fasten the lattice to the 1×2s with $1\frac{1}{4}$-inch decking screws. Attach the reinforced panels to the wall with spacers and screws.

## MAKE YOUR OWN LATTICE

Buy 1×2s or have a lumberyard make 1×1s. Cut the verticals and lay them on a flat surface. Use a tape measure to mark the

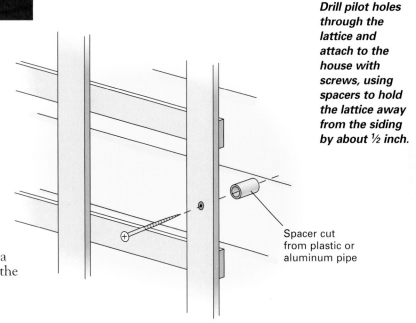

*Drill pilot holes through the lattice and attach to the house with screws, using spacers to hold the lattice away from the siding by about $\frac{1}{2}$ inch.*

Spacer cut from plastic or aluminum pipe

# TRIM AN ENTRY DOOR

If classic moldings are appropriate for the style of your home, use them to add distinction to your entry door. You can now purchase moldings made of high-density urethane. They are available already formed in wide, stately configurations. Urethane moldings will not warp, decay, splinter, mildew, or attract insects. They also are less expensive and easier to install than similar wood molding.

Purchase an entrance system containing pilasters (the vertical pieces) and a decorative lintel (the horizontal cap). For the pilasters, you may need to purchase the upper corner blocks and/or the lower blocks separately. If you buy the pilasters as completely assembled units, be sure that they are the correct length or that you can cut the lower blocks to make them fit. If the lintel is one piece, make sure it, too, is the correct length. If you need to cut it, the tricky part may be making very short pieces on either end of the lintel so it has a finished look. Take the measurements of your door to a lumberyard or home center and ask for everything you need.

You can also use standard wood moldings, stacking various styles on top of or next to one another to produce complex, decorative patterns (*see pages 10–11*).

## INSTALL THE PILASTERS

In most cases, the molding will look best if it covers half the thickness of the door jamb. (The jamb is made of three pieces facing at right angles to the wall; the hinges are attached to it.) Make pencil marks on the jamb to indicate the halfway point and use them when you measure. Cut the pilasters to length, taking into account the bottom and top blocks, if they are separate.

If you have beveled horizontal siding (clapboard), use shims to make a smooth surface for nailing the pilasters. (It is possible simply to nail the pilasters to the siding, but you will have a series of long V-shaped gaps on the outside edges, which will be very difficult to fill with caulk.) Use a chalk line to make vertical lines indicating where the outside of the pilasters will be. Nail shims against the lines. Or install the pilasters first and then insert tight-fitting pieces of trim.

*The door casing is a classic post-and-lintel design, with decorative corner blocks, a raised design on the vertical pieces, and dentiled detail on the horizontal piece.*

## WHAT YOU'LL NEED

**MATERIALS:** urethane molding or wood moldings; shims; galvanized finishing nails or masonry nails or screws; exterior spackle; waterproof construction adhesive; latex/silicone caulk; primer; latex or alkyd exterior paint; mineral spirits, if needed.

**TOOLS:** miter box with backsaw or power miter box; pencil; chalk line; hammer; nail set; caulk gun; putty knife; screwdriver; rags; paintbrushes.

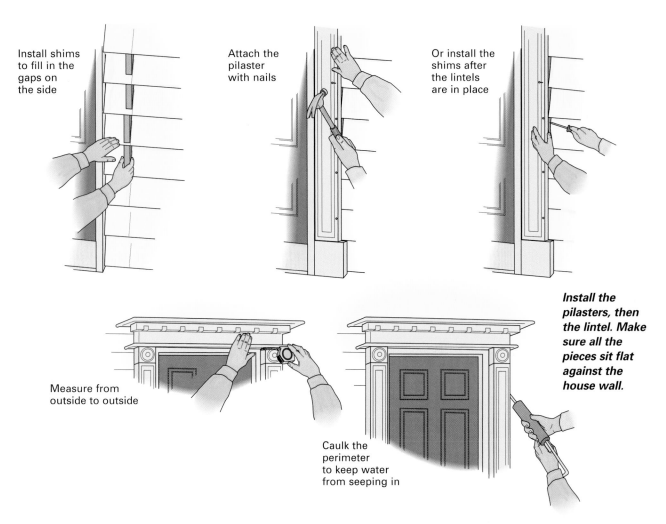

Install shims to fill in the gaps on the side

Attach the pilaster with nails

Or install the shims after the lintels are in place

*Install the pilasters, then the lintel. Make sure all the pieces sit flat against the house wall.*

Measure from outside to outside

Caulk the perimeter to keep water from seeping in

Fit the pieces to make sure they are cut correctly. Using a caulk gun, run a thin bead of construction adhesive on the back of the molding, position it, and drive galvanized finishing nails every foot or so on either side; drive nails into the jamb, as well as the siding.

With wood siding, there is no need to find the studs. If you are connecting trim to a masonry surface, use masonry nails or screws every 2 feet or so on the outside and regular nails to attach to the jamb. Use plenty of construction adhesive.

## INSTALL THE LINTEL

Measure from outside edge to outside edge of the installed vertical molding. It will probably look best to have the lintel overhang the vertical molding by about 1 inch on each side. Cut any lintel pieces, as necessary.

With beveled horizontal siding, you may need to install a long shim at the top, to fill in a gap that you can caulk later. Otherwise, water will seep in, possibly damaging the siding. Buy a piece of beveled siding for this

purpose or mill a piece to fit. Depending on the situation, install the shim before or after you put up the lintel.

Make sure the lintel sits flat against the surface of the house so its face is plumb; if it is at an angle, the job won't look right. Apply construction adhesive, center the lintel, and attach with nails.

## FILL NAIL HOLES, CAULK, AND PAINT

Use a hammer and nail set to poke the nail heads $\frac{1}{4}$ inch or so into the molding. Fill the holes with exterior spackle, using a putty knife or your finger. Allow the spackle to dry and sand smooth.

Apply an even bead of caulk all around the outside edges of the molding. This bead will be very visible, so practice your caulking technique before starting. Apply a smooth, even bead and leave it as is, or use a damp rag to smooth it after applying. Prime, if necessary, and paint with one or two coats of latex or alkyd exterior house paint.

# BUILD A SPLIT-RAIL GATEWAY

A simple, low railing like this will not keep out dogs and thieves, but it will clearly define your property. And it may keep the kids from cutting across the lawn on their bikes. Most importantly, its rustic good looks will welcome people to your house. Building the project will take half a day to a day.

## BUY THE PARTS

A fencing-supply source or home center will have the parts you need. Make sure the rails will fit into the mortises. Select posts that are structurally sound. Sort through the lumber yourself to find sturdy pieces that do not have major cracks and that are fairly consistent in width and thickness.

This fence may endure abuse, so make sure the posts are long enough to provide stability when sunk in the ground.

Lengths of 6 feet will probably be long enough. For extra strength, buy concrete; one 80-pound bag of ready-mix per posthole is plenty.

*A low fence adds rustic beauty and gives your home a warm, friendly look.*

## WHAT YOU'LL NEED

**MATERIALS:** 8 split rails with notched ends; 4 split-rail posts with mortises; 2 lengths of rebar; pea gravel; concrete; paint or sealer/preservative, if needed.

**TOOLS:** posthole digger; wheelbarrow or bucket; hammer; level; string; tape measure; drill; long bit; stakes; scrap lumber; small sledgehammer.

## LAY OUT AND DIG THE HOLES

Pound a couple of stakes in the ground and tighten a string between them to mark the location of the fence. Measure from the front wall to make the fence parallel to the house.

Mark for the inside two posts by digging the postholes. Use a fence rail as a guide to mark for the outside two postholes.

Dig the holes, using a clamshell-type or twist-type posthole digger. If the digging is tough, take your time; many do-it-yourselfers have suffered pain by doing this work. Hiring someone may be a good idea. If you run into small roots, chop them with the posthole digger. For larger roots, you may need to use an axe or a saw. If the root is a large one from a tree, consider moving the fence in order to avoid damaging the tree.

Dig the holes to a consistent depth if the lawn is level. Put a piece of tape or a notch on the posthole digger to indicate the correct depth. If the lawn is not level, you can have the fence follow the slope or use a level on top of a straight board to ensure that the post tops are level with one another.

Dig the holes a couple of inches deeper than they need to be, then shovel in a little gravel, so water can drain away from the bottoms of the posts.

## ASSEMBLE THE FENCE

Set the posts nearest the sidewalk into their holes and temporarily brace them in position by shoving scrap lumber in the hole. Check to see that the posts are fairly plumb.

Slip the rails into the mortises. Set the outside posts in the holes and slip the rails into these mortises. Temporarily brace the outside posts and check for plumb. Slip in the other rails and lay them on top of each other on the ground at the fence ends. You may need to cut the lower end rail to make it come out the same length as the upper one.

## ANCHOR THE FENCE

There are various ways to anchor fence posts. Check with a fence dealer or a neighbor for the one that works best in your area.

■ **SET POST IN CONCRETE:** Check often during this process to be sure the posts stay plumb. In a wheelbarrow or other large container, mix dry concrete mix with enough water so it is barely pourable. Pour into the hole and poke the concrete with a piece of reinforcing bar or thin stick to make sure there are no air bubbles. Mound the concrete slightly above grade, so water will drain away.

■ **SET POST IN TAMPED SOIL:** Shovel in a foot or so of soil, tamp it firmly, and repeat until the hole is filled. Mound the soil a bit so water runs away from the post.

■ **SET POST IN PEA GRAVEL:** Pour in gravel, tamping as you go. Don't mound it up; water will run down through the gravel.

Drill a hole through both end rails—about 6 inches from the grounded end. Use a drill with a long bit that is the same thickness as the rebar. (Or buy a bit extension and attach it to a standard spade bit.) Pound the rebar into the ground until the top is flush with the top of the rail. Dab the exposed end of the rail with brown paint or just let it rust.

If you want the fence to turn gray with time, brush on a clear sealer/preservative. To keep a brown color, use tinted sealer or a sealer that blocks ultraviolet light.

*Assemble the fence, checking that the posts are plumb, then slip in the rails.*

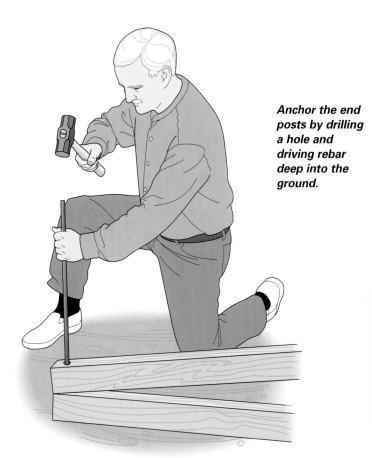

*Anchor the end posts by drilling a hole and driving rebar deep into the ground.*

# INSTALL LANDSCAPE LIGHTS

Low-voltage landscape lights give a house instant beauty. They highlight architectural details, landscape plantings, and special focal points, such as a group of attractive trees. Lights turn decks, patios, terraces, and yards into nighttime living spaces. They also make a yard and house safe and secure by lighting places like steps and approaches to the house.

Safe and worry free, these do-it-yourself 12-volt lighting systems are energy efficient, inexpensive to operate, and they can be installed without conduit, junction boxes, or tools. The fixtures are available in single units and in kits. Installing a system will take a few hours.

*Cheery, yet subtle, low-voltage lights make a house elegant and inviting. They also make paths safer at night.*

## SAFETY LIGHTING

Well, spot, or accent lights can light up house numbers. Bracket lights illuminate front steps and doors. Flood, tier, mushroom, bollard, and post lights illuminate steps, paths, and swimming pools. Post lights help define long driveways and walkways. Floodlight on approaches to a house discourages thieves. Special underwater fixtures can light swimming pools.

## WHAT YOU'LL NEED

**MATERIALS:** low-voltage kit with lights, transformer, stakes, and cable; motion sensor or photovoltaic cell, if needed.

**TOOLS:** tape measure; shovel; pliers; screwdriver.

## LIGHTING EFFECTS

■ **DOWNLIGHTING:** A floodlight mounted high in trees or on the house casts light from above over a broad area. Mounted closer to the ground, it casts light on flower beds, shrubs, walkways, or steps.

■ **DECK LIGHTING:** Compact surface lights mount vertically or horizontally to illuminate deck railings, steps, and benches. Some come with wood trim that can be treated to match the deck; some are especially designed for use on decks.

■ **UPLIGHTING:** Well, spot, and accent lights hidden at the base of trees or other objects throw light upward, highlighting their shape or texture.

■ **MOONLIGHTING:** Floods mounted high in trees filter light down through the branches, casting attractive shadows.

■ **ACCENT LIGHTING:** Mushroom floods spread light on focal points, such as flower beds, creating sparkling islands of light.

■ **BACKLIGHTING:** Well, spot, and accent lights hidden behind bushes bounce light off walls or other surfaces, highlighting their texture or architectural details.

■ **DIFFUSED OR SPREAD LIGHTING:** Mushroom, tier, or bollard lights produce soft, circular patterns on low-level garden beds and paths.

## PLANNING GUIDELINES

Be creative, but don't overlight. You want a balance of light and shadow to create intriguing effects in the yard.

To test different techniques, have family and friends aim flashlights from different directions and at various objects as you study them from a distance. As you plan, remember you want to conceal the light source wherever possible. One exception is decorative spread or accent lights that are meant to be seen.

## HOW LOW-VOLTAGE LIGHTS WORK

At the heart of a low-voltage system is a transformer that reduces standard 120-volt household current to 12 volts. It plugs into a standard electrical outlet. Transformers come in a range of sizes. To choose the right size, add up the watts of all the lamps you plan to use; this is the system's total nominal wattage (TNW). Based on the manufacturer's specifications, choose a transformer with a TNW close to your system TNW. You may need more than one transformer if the system TNW exceeds a certain level, usually about 300 watts.

Buy a transformer with an automatic switch: This can be a timer that automatically turns the lights on and off at preset times, a photocell that turns the lights on at dusk and off at dawn, or a combination of the two. Other options include motion sensors that turn lights on when someone approaches and dimmers that control light intensity.

The low-voltage cable is weather-resistant, self-sealing, and insulated. Determine the size cable you need by the system TNW or by the length of its run. Use 16-gauge cable for installations that don't exceed 150 TNW or a 100-foot run; 14-gauge cable for those up to 200 TNW or 150 feet; and 12-gauge cable for those up to 250 TNW or 200 feet.

The fixtures connect to the cable with a device that pierces the cable and locks in place to wire the light. They install one after another in a series. Use the lamps or lightbulbs recommended by the manufacturer.

## INSTALLING THE SYSTEM

Mount the transformer next to an indoor or outdoor electrical outlet, following the manufacturer's directions. Use the terminal screws to attach the cable to the bottom of the transformer. Plug in the transformer and stretch the cable to its full length.

Lay the cable on the ground under bushes or mulch, or lay it along the foundation. To bury it, cut a slit in the sod at a 45-degree angle, peel back the sod, drop in the cable, and push the sod back in place.

Working from the transformer out to the end of the cable, attach the fixtures to the cable, following the manufacturer's directions. Set or bury the fixtures in the ground or mount them on deck surfaces with screws.

*Most of the work to install a low-voltage system involves running and hiding cable.*

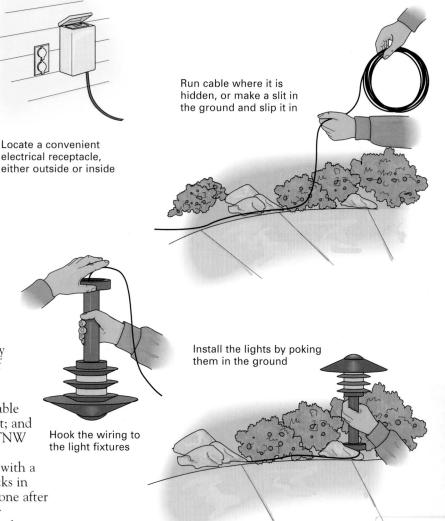

Locate a convenient electrical receptacle, either outside or inside

Run cable where it is hidden, or make a slit in the ground and slip it in

Hook the wiring to the light fixtures

Install the lights by poking them in the ground

# ERECT AN EASY ARBOR

A small arbor set over a front sidewalk or walkway provides a charmingly old-fashioned gateway to a house.

## CHOOSING SIZE AND MATERIALS

*A simple arbor becomes a lush entryway when covered with climbing plants.*

An arbor 5 feet wide, 2 feet deep, and 8 feet high will be ample but not overbearing over a 3-foot-wide sidewalk or path. Use materials that are rot resistant. Heartwood of redwood or cedar works well. Pressure-treated lumber is less expensive and more rot resistant, but many homeowners object to its color. Brown-treated wood (if available in your area) might be a good choice; or plan on painting the structure.

Use 4×4s for the posts, 1×3s for the lattice pieces, and 2×12s or 2×10s for the arched rafters. For a more delicate look, have a lumberyard mill the 4×4s into 3×3s, and use 1×2s for the lattice pieces. Though mostly decorative, the posts should be firmly anchored. Buy posts long enough so you can set them at least 24 inches in the ground.

## LAY OUT, DIG HOLES, AND SET POSTS

Use a framing square and some string with stakes to establish the outside corners of the arbor. Make sure it will be not only parallel to the sidewalk but square, as well.

Dig the holes with a clamshell or twist-type posthole digger. Mark the digger with a piece of tape or notch to indicate the correct depth. Dig each hole a couple of inches deeper than needed, then shovel in a bit of gravel so water will drain away from the post bottoms.

Set the posts in the ground and brace them so they will stay plumb as you work. Cut them to height later. Use pieces of 1×3 or 1×2 as temporary angle braces and stakes. Work with a helper, one person attaching the braces while the other checks that the post remains plumb.

## WHAT YOU'LL NEED

**MATERIALS:** 4×4 posts; 2×10 or 2×12 rafters; 1×2 or 1×3 lattice pieces; gravel; concrete, if needed; 6d galvanized nails or 1⅝-inch decking screws; 3-inch decking screws; primer; paint.

**TOOLS:** posthole digger; step ladder; hammer; drill; level; circular saw; saber saw; tape measure; pencil; string; stepladder; framing square.

Position the braces so they will not get in the way as you attach the lattice pieces.

You could pour the concrete or tamp soil or gravel in the holes at this point. However, you would need to wait a couple of days for the concrete to cure before proceeding, or the posts might become loose as you work. It is best to anchor the posts after the structure is built.

## BUILD THE ARBOR

Using a stepladder and a level set on a straight board, mark the tops of the posts for cutting to the same height. Use a square to draw a line around each post and cut with a circular saw.

Cut the 2×12 or 2×10 rafters to length so they overhang the posts 2 inches on either side. Use a string and a pencil to mark for a smooth curve at the top of one and cut the curve with a saber saw. Use the first piece as a template for marking the second. Have a helper hold each rafter in place while you drill and fasten them to the posts with 5½-inch carriage bolts.

Cut all the side pieces of lattice to the same length, so they overhang the posts 1 inch or so on either side. To attach the lattice, begin with a piece that is 2–3 inches above the ground. Hold it in place, check it for level, and attach it to the posts with 6d galvanized nails or 1⅝-inch decking screws.

To maintain consistent spacing, use a spacer piece of 1×2 or 1×3. Set the spacer on top of the installed lattice piece and the next lattice piece on top of the spacer, and drive screws or nails. Continue working this way until you get to the top.

Cut the overhead lattice pieces so they overhang the rafters by 1 inch. Install the first piece near the edge of the rafters and use the spacer to install the others.

Anchor the posts by pouring concrete, adding tamped soil, or tamping in gravel. *(See page 79 for complete instructions.)*

Finish the arbor by priming and painting it with two coats of high-quality exterior paint. (It will be difficult to repaint after the plants grow.) Or apply a water-repellent finish.

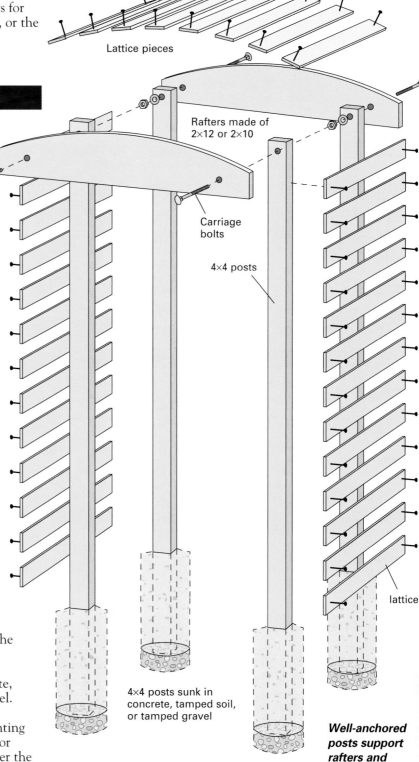

Lattice pieces

Rafters made of 2×12 or 2×10

Carriage bolts

4×4 posts

lattice

4×4 posts sunk in concrete, tamped soil, or tamped gravel

*Well-anchored posts support rafters and horizontal lattice pieces in this simple yet elegant design.*

# ADD A STONE-BORDERED FLOWER BED

A raised flower bed not only serves to show off your flowers by putting them on a pedestal. In addition, it makes gardening easier because you don't have to bend down as far. A variety of natural stone and formed concrete blocks are available to choose from.

The work is simple, but it can be time-consuming and hard on your back. Plan on taking a weekend or two to finish the project.

## MAKE A TRENCH AND FILL WITH GRAVEL

Mark your bed by laying a garden hose around the perimeter. Pour flour or sand on top of the hose, and remove the hose. You'll have a clear line. Dig a trench 2 inches wider than the stones or concrete blocks and 3 inches deep. Fill with 2 inches of gravel and tamp firm with a hand tamper. Add sand to come up almost to grade and smooth out to form a flat surface for the stones or blocks.

## STACK THE STONES

Set the first row of stones or blocks, butted against each other. Set the second and subsequent stones or blocks on top, staggering the joints for strength. To cut a stone or block, make a ¼-inch-deep groove in both sides using a brickset and a hammer. Lop off the waste side with the hammer.

Fill the bed with light topsoil that has plenty of peat moss or other organic material so it will drain easily. During heavy rains, water will seep out through the joints between the stones or blocks.

*A raised bed is simple to build and will show your gardening skills to best advantage.*

Pea gravel

Tamped soil

Brickset chisel

Tamper

Baby sledge

*Dig a trench, fill it with tamped gravel and sand, and stack the stones or blocks. Use a brickset chisel and hammer to cut stones.*

## WHAT YOU'LL NEED

**MATERIALS:** natural stones or concrete blocks; pea gravel; flour or sand; topsoil.

**TOOLS:** shovel; garden hose; hand tamper; hammer or baby sledge; brickset chisel.

# BUILD A TIMBER FLOWER BED

This is a quick way to make a raised bed, and it requires no heavy lifting. Home centers and lumberyards have a variety of large-dimensioned lumber to choose from. Select materials that have proved to be rot resistant in your area.

## FILL A TRENCH WITH GRAVEL

Mark the perimeter of the bed by stretching strings between stakes driven in the ground. If possible, size the bed to minimize cutting of timbers.

Dig a trench 2 inches wider than the timbers and 3 inches deep. Fill with gravel and tamp firm to form a smooth surface almost as high as grade.

## WHAT YOU'LL NEED

**MATERIALS:** railroad ties; 4×4s or other large-dimensioned lumber; pea gravel; 2-foot lengths of rebar; 12-inch spikes; topsoil.

**TOOLS:** circular saw; hand saw; drill; long bit; hand tamper; string; pencil; hammer or baby sledgehammer; framing square.

A timber bed looks great and is easy to build.
Be sure to anchor it firmly to the ground, or the timbers will move out of position after a few years.

## CUT AND LAY THE TIMBERS

Set the first row of timbers in place, ensuring that the corners look neat. To cut the timbers, mark a line around the post using a square. Cut first with a circular saw on all four sides. Finish cutting the inside with a hand saw.

## ANCHOR WITH REBAR AND SPIKES

Every 2 feet or so, drill holes through the timbers, using a long drill bit. Drive the pieces of reinforcing bar through the holes and into the ground, to anchor the timbers.

Stack the second course of timbers on top of the first, staggering the overlap at the corners and leaving at least 2 feet between joints in the middle. Attach these to the first course by pounding in 12-inch spikes every 2 feet or so. Or set the third course in place, drill holes, and drive lengths of reinforcing bar through all three pieces.

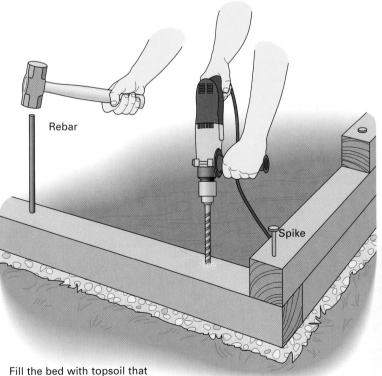

Rebar

Spike

Fill the bed with topsoil that contains plenty of organic material— during a heavy rain, water will seep through the gaps in the timbers

# BUILD A PATIO FLOWER BOX

It may be elementary to build, but this simple wood flower box makes a pleasant addition to a patio, deck, or walkway. It is also portable so it can be moved as needed. Join two boxes—one 10 inches shorter than the other—at right angles, to make a box that fits around corners.

*Flower boxes do not need to be ornate; the plants supply all the decoration you need.*

edge, driving a fastener 1 inch in from each end and at the center. Repeat the procedure on the other side. Attach the end pieces the same way, except drive the end nails ⅜ inch in from the ends.

Cut pieces of 1×2 wood to fit around the bottom of the box, and fasten with glue and nails or screws. Drill pilot holes to avoid splitting the wood. Install the top trim (1×2) the same way, aligning the inside edges of the trim with the inside edges of the box.

Drill six to eight ⅜-inch holes in the bottom of the box for drainage.

Lightly sand the box to prevent splinters. Paint inside and out with two coats of exterior latex paint, letting it dry thoroughly between coats. Or apply a sealer or paint to protect against rot.

Fill the box with 1 or 2 inches of gravel then with light topsoil.

## CUT THE PIECES

Cut 1×10 lumber into three pieces of the same length (30 inches is a good size) for the sides and the bottom of the box. Cut two end pieces, each 11 inches long.

The box has square-cut edges that overlap one another. The sides and ends enclose the bottom, and the end pieces overlap the sides.

## BUILD THE BOX

Apply glue along one edge of the bottom board. Attach another long board at right angles, with all outside edges flush. Turn the side piece face up. Nail or screw the two pieces together along the

## WHAT YOU'LL NEED

**MATERIALS:** redwood, cedar, or pressure-treated 1×10s and 1×2s (rip-cut 1×2s from 1×4s, if needed); polyurethane; glue; 6d galvanized nails or 1⅝-inch decking screws; exterior latex paint or sealer/preservative; gravel; topsoil.

**TOOLS:** tape measure; drill; hammer; square; circular saw; sanding block; 120-grit sandpaper; paintbrush.

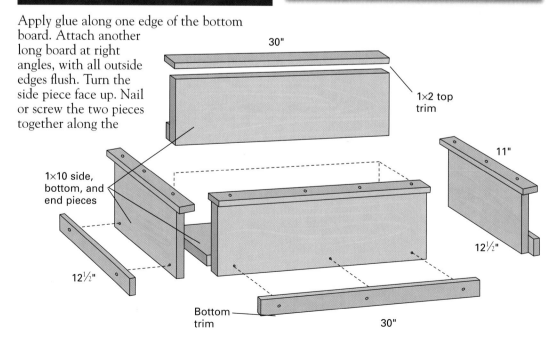

30"

1×2 top trim

11"

1×10 side, bottom, and end pieces

12½"

12½"

Bottom trim

30"

# HANG A FLOWER BASKET

Sometimes a simple addition can make a big difference. With a hanging bracket, you can position flowers exactly where they will be seen to best advantage. And you can change plants at will, showcasing baskets of flowers as they come into full bloom. Making and hanging a bracket will take a few hours.

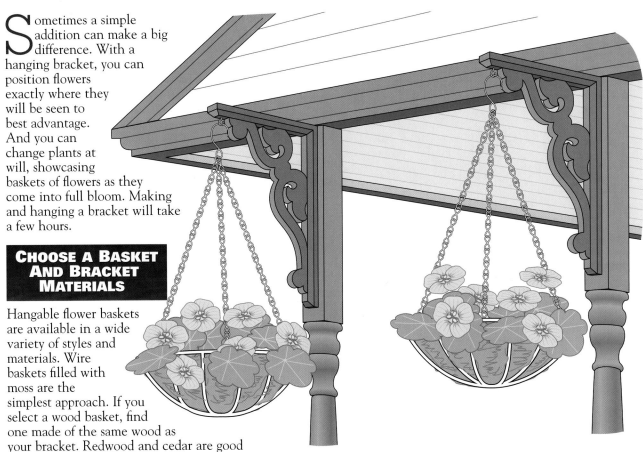

## CHOOSE A BASKET AND BRACKET MATERIALS

Hangable flower baskets are available in a wide variety of styles and materials. Wire baskets filled with moss are the simplest approach. If you select a wood basket, find one made of the same wood as your bracket. Redwood and cedar are good choices. Baskets rarely are finished well so give yours a coat or two of stain or a sealer that blocks ultraviolet light, to keep the wood from turning gray.

You can buy a decorative metal hanging bracket or build one yourself. Choose 2×4 redwood or cedar that is dark in color and has few, if any, knots.

## BUILD THE BRACKET

Cut the wall piece and the arm. The arm should be at least 6 inches longer than the radius of the basket, so the basket will hang

away from the wall. The wall piece can be the same length or slightly shorter.

Make decorative "dog-ear" cuts at one end of both pieces. Use a square to mark for 45-degree cuts that are about 1 inch long.

Set the two pieces on edge on a work surface, with their ends butted and square to each other. Attach the arm to the wall piece by drilling pilot holes and driving 3-inch decking screws. Roughly measure for the angle brace. Cut the brace at 45 degrees at each end and attach it to the arm and the wall piece with 3-inch screws. Paint or apply finish to the bracket. Install a screw-in hook about 2 inches from the end of the arm.

## HANG THE BRACKET

Hold the bracket in position on the wall, checking for level. Drill pilot holes through the bracket and into the wall. Install lag screws with washers by tapping them then screwing them in with a ratchet and socket.

If the wall is masonry, drill only enough to make marks showing the locations. Take the bracket down, drill holes with a masonry bit, and insert lag shields. Drive lag screws into the shields.

*Use brackets in keeping with the style of your house when installing hanging plants.*

## WHAT YOU'LL NEED

**MATERIALS:** hanging flower bucket or wire flower basket; rope or wire; screw-in hook; 2×4 redwood or cedar; 4-inch lag screws with washers; lag shields; 3-inch decking screws; paint or stain and sealer.

**TOOLS:** circular saw; drill; socket and ratchet; masonry bit, if needed; tape measure; square; level; paintbrush.

# CREATE A PATHWAY WITH STEPPING STONES

Stepping stones make a handsome alternative to the traditional garden path. They're also much easier to install because they don't require a gravel base. Lay them in an informal or formal arrangement, as desired, using any number of flat paving materials.

Use a path like this for places that get occasional traffic. It works for mulched areas as well as gardens. The path is awkward when rolling a stroller or wheelbarrow over it, and during rainy weather, it may not be the safest place to walk.

*A walkway that is part lawn and part stone is a graceful way to handle traffic through a yard.*

## WHAT YOU'LL NEED

**MATERIALS:** flagstones, concrete pavers, poured stepping-stones, log slices, or another material that will not crack or rot easily; sand.

**TOOLS:** shovel; gardening trowel; hand tamper or piece of 4×4 or 2×4; garden hose; cardboard; stakes; hammer.

## CHOOSE STEPPING-STONE MATERIALS

There is a wide array of stepping-stone materials. Circles of concrete with exposed aggregate are pleasant. Another inexpensive option is concrete pavers, available in square or octagonal shapes and a variety of colors.

Flagstones create a more natural look; choose stones that tend to be round rather than square and roughly the same size. Large, flat river rocks look great but will be difficult to install. Keep in mind that you need flat surfaces so a lawn mower can go over the stones without damaging the blade.

Log slices are surprisingly durable although they will not last as long as stone or concrete. Don't use them if the lawn stays soggy for long periods.

## ARRANGE THE STONES ON THE YARD

Plan the layout, using garden hose and pieces of cardboard or another movable material to experiment with the general outline of the path and the placement of individual stones. When the layout is decided, drive small stakes into the turf to mark the location of each stone. Count the stones and buy a few more than you need.

Lay the stones in place on top of the lawn in their exact positions. Have members of the family test them. You may need to compromise between the strides of children and the strides of adults.

## CUT THE SOD

Work one stone at a time. With the stone set in place, use a shovel to trace its outline by slicing through the sod around it. With practice, you will make clean, accurate cuts without much effort.

Dig up and remove the turf and any other organic material in each spot, even if that means digging deeply. For each stone, make a hole as deep as the thickness of the stone plus 1 inch. Remove any rocks or other debris from the hole.

## TAMP AND FILL

Use a hand tamper or a piece of 4×4 or 2×4 to tamp the soil firmly. It is important that the soil be firmly compacted, or the stones will shift position over time.

At this point, you could just lay the stones on tamped soil. But adding some sand can make the work easier because the sand will conform to the contours of the stone bottoms more easily than soil will.

Spread 1 inch or so of sand in each bottom and smooth it out. Form a level base or shape the sand to match the bottom of an irregular stone.

## LAY THE STONES

Lay the stone on top of the sand and tamp it down until it is firm and sits level, with its top at about the soil surface so you can run a lawn mower over it.

Keep adjusting until you get the stone just right. It may help to make a gauge by marking a piece of lumber to the correct depth; that way, you can limit the number of times you have to pick up the stones to adjust them.

The stones should not rock or wobble when you step on them. Especially with flagstones, you may need to adjust each stone slightly several times, lifting and filling or removing sand from one spot or another.

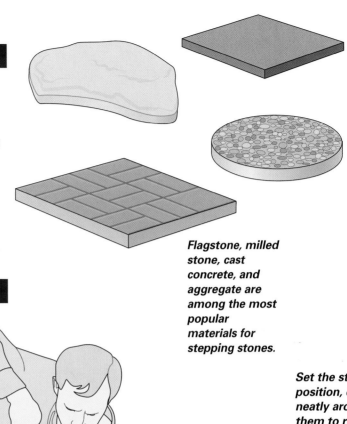

*Flagstone, milled stone, cast concrete, and aggregate are among the most popular materials for stepping stones.*

*Set the stones in position, cut neatly around them to remove the sod, tamp the soil, pour in some sand, and lay the stones.*

# PUT UP A LATTICE PRIVACY SCREEN

A small screen like this is handy for hiding garbage cans or a central air-conditioning unit. It also can help shelter a patio or deck from view.

This design uses a 2×8 lattice sheet that you will cut to length. If you want a larger screen, add another section with another post and a 2-foot-wide lattice sheet. Or space the posts farther apart and make lattice out of 1×2s.

Choose rot-resistant lumber, either pressure-treated or the heartwood of cedar or redwood. It is a good idea to coat the bottoms of the posts, where they will sit in the ground, with a sealer/preservative before you start. Use the thicker type of lattice sheet; it should be at least ¾ inch thick total (each piece of wood should be at least ⅜ inch thick). You will need a day to build the structure here.

*A modest lattice screen nicely hides an unsightly element from view.*

## LAY OUT AND DIG THE POSTHOLES

Lay a straight board on the ground to indicate the location of the screen. It should probably be parallel to a house wall, a sidewalk, or another obvious reference point.

Mark for postholes whose centers are 27 inches apart. This will allow you to set 4×4 posts in the holes with a 2-foot panel spanning the posts.

Dig the holes at least 2 feet deep. Tamp the bottoms firm with a 4×4 and pour a couple inches of gravel into each. Tamp the gravel and set the posts in the holes.

Temporarily brace one of the posts so that it is plumb. Use scraps of lumber driven into the hole or drive stakes into the ground and attach 1×2s to the posts and the stakes.

## ATTACH NAILERS AND LATTICE

Decide how high you want the lattice to extend. The lattice should be held off the ground 2–3 inches; take that into account when you measure. Use a circular saw to cut the 2×8 lattice sheet to the desired length. Cut four 1×1s to the same length.

On the post that is temporarily braced, attach a 1×1 nailer so that the lattice will be centered against the post (*see the top view on page 91*). It should be at the same height you prefer the lattice to be. Use 3-inch decking screws driven every foot or so.

Have a helper hold the lattice against the nailer so one edge butts against the braced post. Attach the lattice to the nailer by drilling pilot holes and driving 4d nails into about every third lattice piece. As you work, rest the lattice on a scrap of lumber on the ground to keep it stable.

## WHAT YOU'LL NEED

**MATERIALS:** 4×4 posts; 2×8-foot lattice sheet; 1×1 nailers; 2×6 rafters; 1×2 braces; wood newels or post caps; 3-inch decking screws; 4d galvanized nails; pea gravel; concrete; paint or preservative.

**TOOLS:** posthole digger; drill; circular saw; hammer; framing square; tape measure; level; pliers; paintbrushes.

Adjust the other post so it aligns with the lattice. Temporarily brace it. Install a nailer with 3-inch screws and attach the lattice with 4d nails just as you did on the first side.

On both posts, complete the lattice sandwich by snugging another 1×1 nailer against the lattice. Drive screws through the 1×1 and into both the post and the other nailer to clamp the lattice in place.

## CUT POST TOPS AND ADD RAFTERS

Use a level to mark the posts for cutting to the same height. On each post, use a square to mark all four sides. Cut with a circular saw.

Cut two 2×6 rafters to 39 inches so they run past the posts 4 inches on either side. Have a helper hold each in place, with the top edge flush with the tops of the posts, while you drive two 3-inch decking screws into each joint. Be sure the rafters overhang the posts the same distance on each side.

## ADD NEWELS

A home center or lumberyard should stock a selection of fanciful newels or decorative post caps to choose from. Get two made of pressure-treated lumber, redwood, or cedar; or use an interior newel and give it several coats of high-quality paint.

The newels may come with their own screws attached; drill pilot holes and twist them into the the middle of the post tops. Otherwise, purchase double-pointed screws. Drill pilot holes in the post top and the newel bottom. Twist the screw into the newel using pliers, then screw it into the post top.

## ANCHOR THE POSTS, PAINT OR FINISH

Verify that the posts are still plumb and rebrace them, if necessary. Secure the posts in the ground by pouring concrete, firmly tamping in soil or tamping in gravel. (*See page 79 for complete instructions.*)

Give the whole structure two solid coats of exterior paint or apply two coats of sealer-preservative containing stain or ultraviolet light blockers.

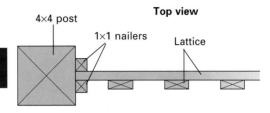

Top view

4×4 post

1×1 nailers

Lattice

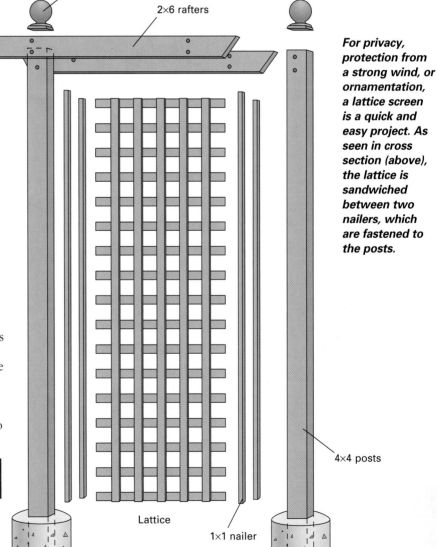

Newel

2×6 rafters

4×4 posts

Lattice

1×1 nailer

*For privacy, protection from a strong wind, or ornamentation, a lattice screen is a quick and easy project. As seen in cross section (above), the lattice is sandwiched between two nailers, which are fastened to the posts.*

# MAKE SHUTTERS AND WINDOW BOXES

If you have plain exterior walls, shutters with a matching or complementary window box will give your home a handcrafted look.

You probably won't put a window box in every window. But by making shutters for all the windows on the most public side

*A combination of window box and shutters brings color and quaint design to an otherwise plain window.*

of your house and by adding a window box or two, you can quickly give your house a unified look.

Use very rot-resistant wood for both the shutters and the window box. Choose high-quality lumber that has been well dried, or your projects may warp during hot weather. A project like this will take about a day.

## MAKE A WINDOW BOX

Small window boxes—no more than 5 inches deep and wide—can simply be screwed into the side of a house. A larger box must be supported from underneath, or it will fall apart and could damage the siding.

The box probably will look most attractive if it is as wide as the window, including the molding. Plan to set it just below the bottom molding of the window, unless you expect to have tall foliage—in that case, set it lower.

Cut the bottom from pressure-treated plywood, and drill a series of $\frac{3}{8}$-inch holes, about 6 inches apart, for drainage. Cut the 1×8 end and side pieces so they fit outside the bottom and cover its edges. Attach the ends and sides to each other and to the bottom, using polyurethane glue and 1$\frac{5}{8}$-inch screws or 6d galvanized nails. Drill pilot holes to avoid cracking the wood.

At a copy center, enlarge one of the patterns on page 93 until it is the size you want for your box. Cut a 1×8 face piece to cover the front of the box. Trace the design on it and cut it out using a drill and a saber saw. Attach the face piece with glue and screws or nails.

Install the 1×2 top trim pieces with their outside edges flush with the outside edges of the box. Miter-cut the corners, and attach by drilling pilot holes and driving 6d galvanized nails or 1$\frac{5}{8}$-inch screws.

Give the box two coats of exterior paint. Fill with 1–2 inches of gravel, followed by light topsoil with plenty of peat moss or other organic matter.

To support the box, purchase decorative brackets (*or make a bracket like the one shown on page 87*); follow the instructions for installing the bracket.

## CHOOSE OR MAKE SHUTTERS

You may find shutters that suit your needs. Vinyl shutters need little maintenance but are available in a limited choice of colors.

To make your own shutters like the ones shown, cut two 1×4s and two 1×2s to the width of the shutter, and two 1×4s to the

## WHAT YOU'LL NEED

**MATERIALS:** ready-made shutters or $\frac{3}{4}$-inch pressure-treated plywood; 1×4s and 1×2s; $\frac{1}{4}$-inch pressure-treated plywood; 1×8s; 1×3s; $\frac{1}{4}$-inch decking screws; 1$\frac{5}{8}$-inch decking screws or 6d galvanized nails; polyurethane glue; latex exterior paint; gravel; topsoil; peat moss.

**TOOLS:** drill; tape measure; framing square; circular saw; saber saw; hammer; paintbrush.

height of the shutter, minus 7 inches. Make the top and bottom pieces by laminating a 1×4 and 1×2 together for each, as shown. Use polyurethane glue, and drive 1¼-inch screws every 6 inches or so. Drill pilot holes to avoid splitting the wood.

Lay the pieces upside down on a work surface, with the 1×2s on top. Position the side pieces to make the complete frame. Measure for the side 1×2s, cut, and attach them as shown, using polyurethane glue and 1¼-inch screws. As you work, check to be sure the sides remain parallel and the corners square.

Cut the plywood to fit in back. Use the template from the window box to mark for cutting a decorative detail. Behind the cut detail, glue a piece of ¼-inch plywood to cover the hole. Cut a horizontal middle piece and glue it in place, driving screws from the back side of the plywood.

Give the shutters at least two coats of exterior latex paint. Attach them using spacers to keep them from touching the siding (*see page 75 for instructions*).

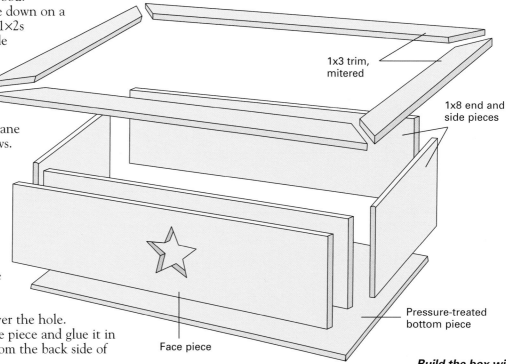

1x3 trim, mitered

1x8 end and side pieces

Pressure-treated bottom piece

Face piece

**Build the box with 1×8 sides and ends, a perforated plywood bottom, and 1×2 top trim.**

**For the shutters, laminate 1×4s with 1×2s to form a frame to fit the plywood. Use a small piece of ¼-inch plywood to cover the decorative cutout.**

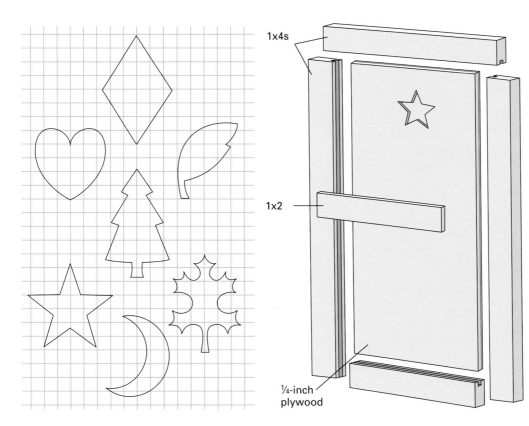

1x4s

1x2

¼-inch plywood

# TILE OVER A CONCRETE SLAB

A dull concrete slab can be made into an enticing patio surface by putting tile on top of it. If installed correctly, a tile surface will last for decades and will require little maintenance.

Choose tiles made for exterior surfaces. Avoid glazed tiles because they will be slippery. Quarry tile makes a good choice, as do flagstone, paving brick, and concrete pavers.

*No one will guess that an unattractive concrete slab lies beneath this striking tile surface.*

## INSPECT AND PREPARE THE CONCRETE

Installing a new tile surface can straighten out a concrete slab but will not add strength. If the old concrete is loose or wobbly, do not tile over it until it has been repaired.

Fill in low spots, cracks, and small holes with patching concrete. To straighten out large areas, combine dry sand with portland cement; mix with water; patch; and trowel smooth. Allow several days for it to cure.

Clean the concrete thoroughly and brush on latex concrete bonder. Allow it to dry.

## LAY OUT THE JOB

Use a chalk line and a framing square or a piece of plywood with two factory edges to establish perpendicular layout lines. Plan well to avoid any slivers at the edges of the patio. If the slab is out of square, try to make it as inconspicuous as possible. (*See page 6 for layout tips.*)

Before you mix the mortar, do a dry run in which you lay out most of the tiles in position to make sure you have chosen the best placement.

## WHAT YOU'LL NEED

**MATERIALS:** tiles, pavers; patching concrete; latex concrete bonder; thinset mortar; sanded grout; plastic spacers.

**TOOLS:** tape measure; chalk line; heavy-duty drill (rentable); mixing bit; tile cutter; tile nippers; wet saw (rentable); mallet; framing square; flat piece of plywood; large paintbrush; notched trowel; laminated grout float; towels; sponge; bucket.

## MIX AND SPREAD ADHESIVE

For a large job, you'll thank yourself for renting a heavy-duty drill that has a mixing blade. Pour the thinset and latex liquid into a 5-gallon bucket, set the mixing blade in, and grip the bottom of the bucket with your feet to keep it from spinning as you run the drill. Mix thoroughly to a toothpaste consistency, let it sit for 10 minutes, then mix again. Have a bucket of water on hand for mixing and to set the blade in when you aren't using it.

Work in 3- to 4-foot-square sections. Do not cover the layout lines. Trowel on a smooth coat, then go over it with the notched part of the trowel. Make grooves but do not let the notches go all the way down to the concrete. Whenever possible, use long, sweeping strokes and keep the surface level.

## SET THE TILES

Lay the tiles instead of sliding them into place. Give each a light tap with a mallet. Use plastic spacers to maintain even grout lines and follow your layout lines precisely.

To make sure you end up with a smooth surface, use a flat piece of plywood about 16 inches square. Periodically, set it on top of the tiles and tap with the mallet.

## CUT TILES

For straight cuts on tiles, a standard tile cutter will do the job (*see page 8 for instructions*).

Making a cutout or notch is more difficult. If you have only a few to make, you can use a tile cutter to cut the tile twice and install two pieces instead of one. You will end up with a hairline joint that is inappropriate for interior surfaces but acceptable for a patio.

If you need to cut pavers or stone, or if you want a more professional-looking cutout or notch, rent a wet tile-cutting saw. It easily and cleanly slices through any masonry material. Always keep the water running on the blade, or it will burn out.

## GROUT AND CLEAN

Allow the mortar to set for a day or two, and remove the plastic spacers. (*See page 8 for instructions on grouting.*) Use the latex additive with the grout. On a large surface, it helps to drag a heavy, wet towel across the surface after the grout has been applied.

Clean the surface with a sponge, watching the grout lines carefully as you work. After everything is dry, buff the surface with a dry cloth.

*Apply a smooth base of mortar first, then comb it with the notched part of the trowel. Work for a smooth, level surface. Use spacers to keep the joint lines consistent.*

*Force the grout into the joints with the float held nearly flat, then tilt the float up to squeegee away the excess.*

# GLOSSARY

**Bevel cut.** A diagonal cut made through the thickness of a board.

**Cable.** Electrical wires wrapped together in a protective metal or plastic sheathing.

**Circuit breaker.** In a service panel, a device that switches off power to an electrical circuit when an overload or short occurs.

**Coped cut.** A profile cut on a piece of molding that allows it to be butted tightly against the face of another piece in an inside corner.

**Flush.** On the same plane as or level with an adjoining surface.

**Glaze.** Paint that is translucent because it has been mixed with water (for latex paint) or glazing liquid (for oil-based paint).

**Grout.** Thin mortar used to fill the joints between tiles.

**Grout float.** A rectangular tool with a soft base used to apply grout.

**Joists.** Horizontal framing pieces, usually regularly spaced, that support a floor or ceiling.

**Lattice.** A pattern of regularly spaced boards, often crisscrossed.

**Miter cut.** A joint formed by two pieces cut to the same angle. Typically, the pieces are cut to 45 degrees to form a 90-degree angle.

**Molding.** Strips of wood, usually small-dimensioned, used to cover exposed edges or as decoration.

**Nail set.** A pencil-like metal tool used to drive the heads of nails slightly below the surface of wood.

**Plumb.** The condition when a board or surface is perfectly vertical.

**Pressure-treated wood.** Lumber or plywood impregnated with a solution that makes it resistant to rot and insect damage.

**Primer.** Special paint used to seal stains and ensure that new paint will adhere to a surface.

**Service panel.** The box into which electricity from the power company flows. It contains fuses or breakers and distributes power in circuits throughout the house.

**Spackle.** A paste that dries and can be sanded after application. It fills cracks and holes in walls.

**Square.** Surfaces positioned at a 90-degree angle to each other.

**Stop valve.** A valve installed near a plumbing fixture to shut off water only to that fixture.

**Studs.** Regularly spaced vertical framing pieces, usually 2×4, to which the wall surfaces (drywall or lathe and plaster) are affixed.

**Thinset mortar.** An adhesive made of cement, fine sand, latex bonding agent, and water.

**Threshold.** A strip of metal or wood attached to a floor to make the transition between two surfaces.

**Transformer.** A device that reduces or increases voltage.

**Underlayment.** Sheets of plywood used to provide a smooth surface for finish flooring.

## METRIC CONVERSIONS

| U.S. Units to Metric Equivalents | | | Metric Units to U.S. Equivalents | | |
| --- | --- | --- | --- | --- | --- |
| To Convert From | Multiply By | To Get | To Convert From | Multiply By | To Get |
| Inches | 25.4 | Millimetres | Millimetres | 0.0394 | Inches |
| Inches | 2.54 | Centimetres | Centimetres | 0.3937 | Inches |
| Feet | 30.48 | Centimetres | Centimetres | 0.0328 | Feet |
| Feet | 0.3048 | Metres | Metres | 3.2808 | Feet |
| Yards | 0.9144 | Metres | Metres | 1.0936 | Yards |
| Square inches | 6.4516 | Square centimetres | Square centimetres | 0.1550 | Square inches |
| Square feet | 0.0929 | Square metres | Square metres | 10.764 | Square feet |
| Square yards | 0.8361 | Square metres | Square metres | 1.1960 | Square yards |
| Acres | 0.4047 | Hectares | Hectares | 2.4711 | Acres |
| Cubic inches | 16.387 | Cubic centimetres | Cubic centimetres | 0.0610 | Cubic inches |
| Cubic feet | 0.0283 | Cubic metres | Cubic metres | 35.315 | Cubic feet |
| Cubic feet | 28.316 | Litres | Litres | 0.0353 | Cubic feet |
| Cubic yards | 0.7646 | Cubic metres | Cubic metres | 1.308 | Cubic yards |
| Cubic yards | 764.55 | Litres | Litres | 0.0013 | Cubic yards |

To convert from degrees Fahrenheit (F) to degrees Celsius (C), first subtract 32, then multiply by $\frac{5}{9}$.

To convert from degrees Celsius to degrees Fahrenheit, multiply by $\frac{9}{5}$, then add 32.